# BOONE COUNTY
## ORIGINALS

Scheidenhelm's drawing of Fred Schulte's glove, Hairbreadth Harry's shoes and Judi Ford's crown. *Courtesy Kit Scheidenhelm.*

# BOONE COUNTY ORIGINALS

## Remarkable PEOPLE AND CURIOUS INCIDENTS

MIKE DOYLE

Charleston · London
THE History PRESS

Published by The History Press
Charleston, SC 29403
www.historypress.net

Copyright © 2010 by Mike Doyle
All rights reserved

First published 2010

Manufactured in the United States

ISBN 978.1.59629.938.2

Library of Congress Cataloging-in-Publication Data

Doyle, Mike, 1948-
Boone County originals : remarkable people and curious incidents / Mike Doyle.
 p. cm.
 ISBN 978-1-59629-938-2
1. Boone County (Ill.)--History--Anecdotes. 2. Boone County (Ill.)--Social life and customs-
-Anecdotes. 3. Boone County (Ill.)--Biography. 4. Curiosities and wonders--Illinois--Boone
County. I. Title.
 F547.B65D69 2010
 977.3'29--dc22
 2010025550

*Notice*: The information in this book is true and complete to the best of our knowledge. It is offered without guarantee on the part of the author or The History Press. The author and The History Press disclaim all liability in connection with the use of this book.

All rights reserved. No part of this book may be reproduced or transmitted in any form whatsoever without prior written permission from the publisher except in the case of brief quotations embodied in critical articles and reviews.

*This book is dedicated to all of us Boone County originals, especially one of the newest ones, my grandson, Jackson Doyle Denning, who was born on May 23, 2010.*

# Contents

| | |
|---|---|
| Preface | 9 |
| Introduction | 11 |
| "No Better Spot on Earth than Little Boone" | 13 |
| "The Hand of God" | 21 |
| The Legend of Big Thunder | 33 |
| The Railroad Arrives | 47 |
| "I Was a Soldier!" | 55 |
| Crimes, Crime Fighters and Strange Legends | 69 |
| Hairbreadth Harry, the King of the s | 77 |
| The Eldredge: The Little Car that Couldn't | 85 |
| "Hundreds of Heroes" | 95 |
| "Our Miss America" | 105 |
| A Major Leaguer | 113 |
| More Boone County Originals | 119 |
| Bibliography | 135 |
| Index | 139 |
| About the Author | 143 |

# Preface

This book began with an e-mail I received from Wally Haas, editorial page editor of the *Rockford Register Star*, in August 2009. I have written a weekly column for the *Register Star* about people, places and things in Boone County since the summer of 1995, and many of those columns told stories about interesting people from our past. Haas forwarded an e-mail from Ben Gibson, a commissioning editor from The History Press in Charleston, South Carolina. The History Press publishes books about specific topics and places and seeks local writers and authors. Because Boone County had a great number of interesting stories to tell, it seemed like a good match.

This book could not have been created without the help of many sources, beginning with George Gibson, former president of the Boone County Historical Society, who turned me on to many of these interesting stories when I visited the museum as a reporter. Through his help and ability to find the most interesting nuggets in the most obscure places, I began to put stories of these Boone County originals in my weekly *Register Star* column. Most of the stories in this book first appeared in this column, which was originally called "Boone County Voices" when it appeared beginning in the summer of 1995. Perhaps the most important thing Gibson did for me and for our local history was to ask me to become a board member of the Boone County Historical Society. Through that service, I met fellow historians like Betty Wright, Beth Luhman, Jack Wolf, Jerry and Carol Rowe, Gary Turner, Don Ellingson and too many others for me to list. I also learned a great deal about the Native Americans who lived in Boone County before the Black Hawk War from the late Roger Gustafson, who helped establish the Boone County Conservation District.

# Preface

When I started doing research for this book, I called on Mary Hale and Lonna Bentley of the Boone County Historical Museum, both of whom kept doors open for me after the museum was closed. I'd also like to thank Lonna for all of her help in finding and saving many of the images that appear in this book. More thanks goes to Marge Hinrichs of the local history room at the Ida Public Library, along with Martin Johnson, who can usually be found there; and others, including Frank Crawford, George Thomas, Bob Lear and Anna Ralston. I'd also like to thank the museum board members who approved of my use of their facilities. That list includes Carol Rowe, Lear, Turner, Crawford, Dick Stegemann, Judy Ernest, Don Banks, Marge Hindert, Steve Anderson, John Wolf, Sam Larson, Ann Bennett, Judy Winter, Peggy Wolf and Andy Ward. Special thanks goes out to three local artists—Gary Simon, local artist and proprietor of the Brick Coffee House and Art Gallery; Kit Scheidenhelm, former art teacher at Belvidere High School; and Troy Yunk, art teacher at Belvidere North High School and formerly at Belvidere High School. I would also like to acknowledge Linda Grist Cunningham, of the *Rockford Register Star*, who selected me to write the Boone County column in 1995 and then encouraged me to continue to write it after I left the newspaper in 1999 to become a journalism teacher in the Belvidere school district. Still more thanks is owed to the people I met along the way.

*Boone County Originals* was not written as a comprehensive book of Boone County history. Its purpose from the start has been to tell about some of the remarkable people and curious incidents that make our county so interesting, despite its small size.

# Introduction

Big Thunder Park is a traditional town square park in the middle of Belvidere, the county seat and largest city in Boone County, Illinois. The park is home to handsome oak trees, open spaces, a playground, a bandstand (where local high school bands often play) and, in the northwest corner, a tall monument. The structure heralds the sacrifices made by Boone County's soldiers and sailors of the Civil War, and local legend tells that it is located on the burial place of Big Thunder, the Potawatomi Indian chief.

Big Thunder's memory resonates in the county's history. Besides a park bearing his name, there is a road and a commercial development that features a sculpture of a Native American that many call Big Thunder. That makes him the first Boone County original, one of the many people whose stories will be told in these pages. Like many of the originals, his story will be wild and fascinating but also enigmatic, because there is little proof that he actually lived.

Boone County, one of the smallest counties in Illinois, has a rich and diverse history despite its size. It was named after Daniel Boone, a man who never set foot on its rich soil, and its most famous legend of Chief Big Thunder may have been a product of the imagination of one of its earliest settlers, Simon P. Doty.

Big Thunder and Simon P. Doty are just two of the many men and women who lived and died in this county at the very top of Illinois. Some of these people moved here and stayed, while some moved on. Some became lifelong natives, while some who were born here stayed only long enough to leave a story that can be told today. All of these people can be called Boone County originals for what they left behind.

# "No Better Spot on Earth than Little Boone"

Simon P. Doty was more than an original settler of Boone County, Illinois. Doty was the first elected sheriff, albeit for a short time, and housed the first county jail in his home. He built one of the county's first frame houses, and as manager of the first hotel and tavern, he got the first liquor license in Boone County. When the first county election was held in 1836, his home was a polling place.

His impact ranged beyond northern Illinois, as well, for he was the first person in the county elected to the state legislature in Springfield. Although it was said that he could neither read nor write, he had a quick wit, which was needed then because representatives from the more established population centers in central and southern Illinois looked down on the newcomers in the far north.

According to Devillo Hall, a contemporary of Doty's, one representative from southern Illinois "sneered" at Doty's portion of the state, saying it "froze up" in winter.

Doty had a quick reply.

"I must tell you a dream of one of my constituents," Doty said.

> *Oliver Hale dreamed he was dead and was approaching the great gate. He timidly knocked, and St. Peter called out, "Who's there?"*
>
> *He answered, "Oliver Hale."*
>
> *"Hale?" said St. Peter. "I never heard the name. Where from?"*
>
> *"Boone County, Illinois."*
>
> *With that, St. Peter looked at his map and said, "Go back, Oliver Hale, to Boone County. That is a better country than this."*

# BOONE COUNTY ORIGINALS

Simon P. Doty, one of the county's original settlers. He was the first sheriff and the first state representative. *Courtesy of the Boone County Historical Museum.*

And so begins our story about Little Boone County, one of Illinois' smallest counties but one that is large in home-grown characters, often with tall tales, who have become our own originals.

Boosterism like Simon Doty demonstrated didn't go out of style in Boone County. In 1926, when the movie *Belvidere's Hero* was filmed locally, a spokesman for the movie's producers said, "The city of Belvidere has great film possibilities and scenic beauty that equals the famed wonders of California's sea coast."

In the 1930s, when honest men rode the rails during the Depression, Boone County had an original hobo in Hairbreadth Harry. A true "Knight of the Road," he loved his native Belvidere and boasted of it in his poetry.

"I'll tell you I'm treated kindly in Belvidere, Illinois, beautiful city, home of Hairbreadth Harry, pretty girls and clever men," Harry wrote in his book, *The Life, History, and Poetry of Hairbreadth Harry* (or *Old Inner Tubes Comes Clean*).

To understand what is original about Boone County, we must first look to its past. And through the bits and pieces of stories, historical data, anecdotes, local legends and other sources, it is possible to build a framework that tells many of the tales of our county. We were part of the Northwest Territories, originally a far-flung part of Ohio. When the states were originally mapped out, our area was to be part of Wisconsin, and even after we became part of Illinois, there was an effort to secede and rejoin Wisconsin. We were also once part of Winnebago County but broke off on our own and then had to settle another small border controversy.

Boone County was named in honor of the great frontiersman and pioneer Daniel Boone. It has been the home of Indian legends, a major-league

# Remarkable People and Curious Incidents

baseball player, a Miss America, a cross-dressing Civil War soldier, a world-class hobo and a direct *Mayflower* descendent, among others.

Its landform of mostly prairie and some rolling hills took shape from the Wisconsinan Glacier from the last ice age. Before the glacial upheaval, a large canyonlike depression cut through the center of the county. The material left after the glaciers resulted in several quarries.

While it may not have been a regular gathering place for Indians, there is solid evidence that natives, mostly members of the Potawatomi tribe, traveled through, camping, hunting, fishing and probably planting some crops. Boone County's location along the northern border of Illinois and Wisconsin made it a natural route for Native Americans moving between Lake Michigan and the Mississippi River, two major waterways in the Great Lakes region.

The name *Potawatomi* appears to be of Chippewa origin, meaning "People of the Place of Fire." They may have been part of a larger tribe made up of Chippewa and Ottawa Indians. These people moved into the upper part of lower Michigan until the Potawatomis were forced to move farther west, into northeastern Wisconsin and, eventually, southeastern Wisconsin and northeastern Illinois. One of the larger Potawatomi settlements is near the present-day city of Milwaukee. Potawatomi people moved freely throughout the region and often stopped from time to time in Boone County.

Historical evidence exists of Native American campgrounds in Boone County. Two are located in Spring Township in the southeastern corner on high places and two along waterways. The most intriguing former campground is located south of Capron, where Angling Road meets County Line Road adjacent to McHenry County. Another was a place where they would meet to trade goods and information, located along the Kishwaukee River in Spencer Park on the western edge of Belvidere. There is evidence that Indians hunted here; artifacts, such as arrowheads, have been discovered. Many of these arrowheads were found in the wet prairie area of eastern Boone County, where the Kishwaukee flows from McHenry County. These Native Americans did trap beaver, trading with Europeans possibly as early as the 1580s, with Jacque Cartier. Most of their trading appears to have been with the Sauk Indians in the Rock Island area. That trading route could easily have followed the Kishwaukee, which feeds into the Rock River south of Rockford. The Rock then flows into the Mississippi at Rock Island.

The Potawatomis cherished four sacred plants: sage, sweet grass, cedar and tobacco. They would burn sage and then smudge it on their faces to ward off negative spirits. Sweet grass, native to wet prairies such as those found in eastern Boone County, was used for braiding. When burned, it created an aroma that was said to call upon good spirits. Cedar was strong wood and was used to call the attention of the creator. Tobacco was the most powerful of their plants; it was sacred and strong.

The geography of the area also played a part in the regular activities of the early people. Illinois was well known for its prairies, giving us one of our state's nicknames: "the Prairie State." Prairie fires were common and were often set by Native Americans to foster new plant growth. One large prairie fire occurred long before the European settlement and was overwhelming in its scope. Fueled by a strong, dry southwestern wind, it began near Peoria and burned the prairie northward for more than 130 miles until it was stopped on the western bank of the Rock River in present-day Rockford.

Boone County is transitional in its geography. Its southern half is generally flat and featureless, which is indicative of the northernmost expanse of the state's great prairie. In the northwestern corner of the county, the Native Americans traversed hills and forests, the beginning of the woodlands that dominate Wisconsin to the north. The prairie suited the Potawatomis in Boone County. The early people were hunters and gathers, but over time, Native Americans came to use what the land would provide, growing the "three sisters"—corn, beans and squash. They planted in the spring, using downed trees or branches for vines, and visited their prairie gardens two more times in the growing season—in August for green or sweet corn, and in

Indian Directional Tree. *Photo taken from the book* Boone County: Then and Now.

# Remarkable People and Curious Incidents

Sign showing the former location of the Fern Hill Indian campground. *Photo by author.*

the late fall to harvest the beans, squash and pumpkins. These gardens were not very large, but they were productive.

Two of the sites of former Indian campgrounds are in Spring Township, in Boone County's southeasternmost corner. One was located on a small rise near Huber Road and Shattuck Roads; the other on Fern Hill, the highest spot on southern Boone County. The most recognized former Indian campground is near the present-day County Line Cemetery on a small rise on an oxbow of Piscasaw Creek. With high ground near water, it was a perfect site for an Indian campground. Another clue to its former use was located to the west of the campground. It was a tree that stood for an estimated three hundred years, falling to the ground in 2008. It was known in Boone County as the Indian Directional Tree.

Directional or trail trees were commonly found in the thick forests of eastern and southeastern native lands before the arrival of the Europeans and were used to point out routes, as well as the location of food and game. Altering growth of plants was common, and Native Americans probably used weights or bent limbs so plants would grow and point in the intended

Sign showing the former location of an Indian campsite. *Photo by author.*

direction. The Boone County tree was a red oak with a limb low to the ground that grew straight out from the trunk. Trail trees had been identified in about a dozen locations in northern Illinois, including Lake County. One existed in Zion in Lake County until the late 1990s. These trees were used by Native Americans who circled around the southern end of Lake Michigan. Boone County's trail tree could have been altered early in the eighteenth century to point travelers to the nearby campsite. They were natural directional signs.

Other landmarks of Native Americans are long gone but remain part of local history. Three Indian mounds were found along Grange Hall Road, and nearby stood an oak tree with its center hollowed out. It was said to be an Indian "message tree."

Although Native Americans were not permanent residents before the arrival of the Europeans, it appears that some of their traditions left permanent marks. One trader, Joseph Thiebeau of the American Fur Co., trapped land that he owned or claimed on the east side of the Rock River. At the time, Boone County was part of Winnebago County, and some of the land he worked was in Boone.

# Remarkable People and Curious Incidents

When the Europeans began to trickle in, they adapted some of the place names to the waterways, such as Kinnikinnick and Piscasaw Creeks and Kishwaukee River. In the original government survey of the area, Piscasaw is spelled "Piskasaw," which has clear ties to the Native Americans. Most sources believe that the creek is named after the Potawatomi word for buffalo. Kinnikinnick has links to a Chippewa word for mixing, but it also appears to be the name for Indian tobacco, a mixture of prepared plants, including the plant called Kinnikinnick. That place name continues today in Kinnikinnick Conservation Area.

Kishwaukee appears to have a more romantic origin. One definition is that it means "place of the sycamores" or "free from storms," but another source, described in the *Belvidere Standard* in 1853, is much more interesting. According to the newspaper, an ash tree near the river that bisects Boone County from east to west had a striking resemblance to a tree in the legend of a Pawnee Indian woman named Kish-wa-kee. Using information from *Gleason's Pictorial Journal*, the tree was seen by many early stagecoach travelers

Local artist Gary Simon's drawing of the Indian directional tree, formerly located south of Capron. *Courtesy Gary Simon.*

who were familiar with a Pawnee legend that a woman was transformed into a single tree. The newspaper reported that the maiden was to have "possessed uncommon beauty, though her form and feature were scarcely feminine." In a family dispute, she killed an Indian chief, Manatou, who was about to be wed. When his young bride, Euruqua, was summoned and asked what should be Kish-wa-kee's fate, Euruqua said, "Let her still live." But Oronoo, the eldest of the tribe, decreed that she would have to die. Upon hearing her fate, Kish-wa-kee dove into the nearby river and was never seen again. On the spot where she was condemned and from which she dove into the water, a tree soon appeared, "whose outlines bore so strong a resemblance to her distorted features that none who gazed upon it doubted that it was the wretched woman."

The site of this tree that gave the Kishwaukee its name has been lost to history. One possible location is where the Native Americans forded the Kishwaukee because a limestone outcropping made for an easy crossing. This river crossing would eventually be known as Cline's Ford.

While there is little in the way of contemporary histories of two local Indian chiefs, their names live on today in Belvidere. The first is Menomonee, who it is said was the chief of the Potawatomi Indians when the first Europeans arrived. His people may have numbered about seventy, and their cemetery was said to have been located on the north bank of the Kishwaukee River, near the present-day Apollo Activity Center. There are no other documented traces of Chief Menomonee in Illinois, although there was a Potawatomi village with that name in Indiana.

The other Indian chief, and another significant event, changed the landscape of county history forever in the first half of the nineteenth century. The event was the Black Hawk War. The chief was Big Thunder.

# "The Hand of God"

Illinois became a state in 1818, settled primarily in its south and central parts. Most of the land in the northern and northwestern parts of Illinois was unsettled frontier, aside from some trapping along the abundant rivers and lead mining in the Galena area of northwestern Illinois. By 1827, the state was impatient and petitioned the federal government for the removal of Native Americans in the area. That land was deeded to the state in an 1804 treaty with the Sac and Fox tribes, but one Sac warrior, Black Hawk, refused to accept the treaty.

Black Hawk was born at the mouth of the Rock River near present-day Rock Island and loved the river valley where his ancestors had lived. During the War of 1812, he sided with the British in the hopes of regaining his land, but the British never had any intention of helping the Indians in their quest. By 1830, most of the Sac and Fox people had moved to reservations in Iowa, and in 1831, the state forced Black Hawk to sign an agreement that he would not cross back into Illinois. Over the winter of 1831–32, Black Hawk received false reports that Canadian tribes were willing to move south and aid in his quest for his tribe's lost land. So he crossed the Mississippi River in April 1832 with his followers, including women and children, and moved northeast up the Rock River Valley in defiance of the state.

A state militia was organized to confront the band, and among those who volunteered were two men who would play significant roles in the Civil War. They were Abraham Lincoln, who became our sixteenth president, and Jefferson Davis, the first and only president of the Confederacy. This was Lincoln's only true military experience, and it wasn't very memorable.

He always seemed to arrive a day after any significant skirmishes and more than once said that the only blood he saw during service was that from mosquito bites.

The war was taken quite seriously, however, as the militia chased Black Hawk north along the Rock River and into Wisconsin, where things ended tragically at the Battle of Bad Axe. One of the local developments of the war effort came when the state requested regular army troops. As a result, General Winfield Scott, who would become a military hero in the Mexican War in 1842 and the first commander of Union forces in the Civil War, led a band of army regulars from Chicago to intercept Black Hawk's band in Wisconsin. Scott's troops never caught up with the Indians, but there are many accounts of his passing through northern Illinois.

Records of the War Department show that General Scott was at his headquarters in Chicago on July 29, 1833, and that his troops were at Dixon's Ferry in early August and at Fort Armstrong near Rock Island in late August. Local stories tell that General Scott led his army regulars on a trail that is Genoa Road today, across the Kishwaukee River and then northwest in pursuit of the Indians. Scott may have split his forces, or the troops that came through Boone County may have been volunteers. However, in the years after the Black Hawk War, some of his former troopers are said to have made their way through the area and recalled that the army crossed the Kishwaukee River at its northernmost bend in what would become Belvidere. A street name near that river bend bears the name Scott's Army Trail, in recognition of the historical trek through Boone County. Many of the old histories of the county tell of pioneers following Scott's Army Trail from Chicago to Boone County. From the river crossing, Scott's troops reportedly camped in a wooded area on high ground northwest of present-day Belvidere. That area is believed to be where Caledonia Road crosses Beaver Creek.

The story of Scott's trek through Boone County got some credence from Asher Jenner, who opened the first watch repair shop between Chicago and Galena in 1838. Jenner's shop was located in John Towner's hotel, and he recalled that after the Black Hawk War, General Scott came through Belvidere on the Frink and Walker Stage and stayed at the hotel. Jenner, a musician who played the clarinet, was joined by other musicians who performed for General Scott. After enjoying the music, General Scott talked to the men and told them he recalled passing through the area during the Black Hawk War. He told Jenner that he saw the place where the army forded the Kishwaukee River and could see where the banks still showed the ruts where artillery pieces passed through. The location of Scott's Army

# Remarkable People and Curious Incidents

Trail today may not be on the actual trail the men used, but it serves as a monument to them, nonetheless.

The Black Hawk War had an even greater impact in Boone County. As a result of the last Indian conflict in Illinois, land was opened up for settlement, and it didn't take long for the new Americans to find their way to what was to become Belvidere and Boone County. What the first white settlers discovered was a prairie that was well watered and featured abundant woodlands. Two of the county's townships are named after significant features—Flora Township after the fruitful prairie flowers and Spring Township after the number of natural springs. Although there wasn't an abundance of game, there is evidence that buffalo roamed our gently rolling lands. Piscasaw Creek in eastern Boone County may have been named after a Native American word for buffalo. In addition, there was evidence of a number of buffalo wallows in that part of the county.

Although the first Europeans to set foot in Boone County probably were trappers seeking beaver, they didn't have a mind to settle down. The next great wave of Europeans was not as interested in trapping. Instead, they were seeking land to cultivate and rivers to harness for milling. But it wasn't all milk and honey. The first settlers found Boone County to be about half prairie and half woodlands and wooded groves. Those first to arrive took the land along the rivers and creeks. These barrens or oak savannahs provided land, as well as wood and water. After those areas were staked, the prairies, thought at first to be worthless, were settled.

The first of the pioneers began to arrive in 1835, three years after the Black Hawk War. They included John Langdon, whose family built a cabin in the southeast corner of Long Prairie. Langdon's wife died in the winter of 1837–38, one of the first deaths of original pioneers. Another was Livingston Robbins, who came with his brothers from Chautauqua County, New York. Robbins didn't stay long, and neither did Archibald Metcalf and David Dunham, who purchased Robbins's claim. Also in 1835, John K. Towner was heading toward Chicago from Michigan when he met up with Cornelius Cline and Erastus Nixon. Cline and Nixon were headed toward Rockford, a promising settlement at the banks of Kent Creek and the Rock River. They probably followed the trail blazed by General Winfield Scott a few years earlier but never got to the Rock River. Instead they came upon the Kishwaukee River, where they found Metcalf and Dunham living in a small shanty on their claim.

Towner, Cline and Nixon arrived in June when the slopes around the river were covered with flowers, including wild roses. After staying the night,

Towner is said to have told his traveling companions, "Others, expecting to find a paradise on the Rock River, may go there; as for me, I go no further." Nixon and Cline agreed, and they stayed. Towner built a log cabin and then returned for his family in Michigan. When they made the trek east, they stopped in Chicago, where Towner bought four pair of oxen and a prairie schooner. While Towner walked the oxen, Mrs. Towner drove the wagon. At midnight on July 31, 1835, the small band stopped for good at the southern banks of the Kishwaukee.

Mrs. Towner's arrival made her the first European woman in Boone County. Although most of the Indians found by the original settlers were friendly, there were stories of rogues, including one who threatened Mrs. Towner shortly after she arrived. She and her children were alone in their cabin when an intoxicated Indian entered it and said he was going to kill her. Mrs. Towner answered that she was going to kill him. When one of her daughters, a ten-year-old, said there was a loaded gun in the house, the Indian responded by grabbing a knife from his belt—a knife, Mrs. Towner said later, that looked as big as a sword. Because of his drunken state, the Indian lost the advantage, and Mrs. Towner was able to push him out the door and bar it. But the door wasn't solid and had spaces large enough for the Indian to thrust his knife through several times. When that didn't satisfy him, he climbed onto the roof and tried to climb down the mud-and-stick chimney. But Mrs. Towner's quick thinking worked again as she ripped open a straw bed and fed the fire to the chimney. By this time, the Indian had given up, and the noise caused men in the area to come to her rescue.

The extreme hardships are hard to imagine, but Mrs. Towner told of another one that she witnessed. She believed that the wife of one of the Potawatomie chiefs was of European origin. The woman was painted to conceal her identity, but Mrs. Towner told others that the chief's wife would often come to visit. On one of those visits, the woman played with the Towners' youngest child. As the woman was tickling the child's chin, she began to use English words, "Bubby, bubby." Mrs. Towner noticed this and approached the woman, telling her she knew how to talk to and handle white babies. From that moment on, the woman never spoke another word, and the Indians were moved west across the Mississippi River.

The extreme southwestern township of Flora was settled in 1835 by Arthur Blood, who erected two log cabins in a wooded area directly east of what is known today as Blood's Point Cemetery. Although Blood did not stay long in the county, the cemetery that bears his name would become the stuff of local legends. Because he was the first European on the land, Blood

## Remarkable People and Curious Incidents

and others were able to lay claim to the gently rolling prairie. According to local legends, the first people to use the land would lay claim in the following way: A settler would stake out a point and then aim his oxen and plow in a straight row in one direction (perhaps west toward the setting sun) for the length of the day. On the second day after staking a claim, the settler would take a ninety-degree turn and plow in that direction (perhaps south). Then, on the third day, he would do the same and turn another ninety degrees, east in this case, and continue until a section of equal size was created. The size of the claim was determined by the belief that any point was reachable from the center and that most of the claim could be worked in a day.

History tells us that John Handy was the first to settle in Spring Township on Boone County's southeastern corner. Handy came west from Ohio, arriving in 1835 to build a home east of the intersection of Genoa and Reeds Crossing Roads. Handy's homesite is preserved to history with a sign noting that he was the first settler in the area in 1835. Handy eventually became the county's first coroner in 1837, and his traveling companion established roots that continue today.

Sign showing the location of John Handy's homesite. Handy was one of the first settlers in Spring Township. *Photo by author.*

Shattuck's Grove Cemetery, established when a traveler died in the barn of the original settlers. *Photo by author.*

Arriving with Handy was Erastus Shattuck, who was joined by his brother, Alfred, and his son, Harlan. These original Shattucks came from Painesville, Ohio, and staked a claim two miles east of Handy's. Called Shattuck's Grove, it was located along an old Indian trail, and some stories have been told that the first Shattucks were often harassed by Native Americans, who had two campgrounds nearby. One was south of the Shattuck homestead on a small hill; the other was northwest on the high point of Fern Hill Road. West of the Shattuck homestead is Shattuck's Grove Cemetery. Established in 1840, its first permanent resident is said to have been a stranger who was given shelter by the Shattucks one night. When the family went to find him the next day, he was discovered dead in the loft. Shattucks have made their home in Boone County since those early days.

# Remarkable People and Curious Incidents

In the fall of 1835, General James Sawyers claimed land on Beaver Creek about a half mile upstream from the Kishwaukee River in the western extreme of the county. There he built the first mill in the region, and it became a significant place for the early settlers to gather. In a short time, he added a gristmill and plotted the settlement that was known as Sayresville and Cleveland before it became Newburg. Newburg appeared to be in the right location for growth and, in time, was the site of a chair factory; a wool carding mill; a two-story tavern known as the Newburg House, or Halfway House, because it was halfway between Rockford and Belvidere; and a distillery, which lives on today in the name of the nearby road. However, fate, circumstance and William Holt Gilman were not kind to Newburg, and it was lost to history.

Rollinsville is another settlement given ghost-town status. John Quincy Rollins established the place with his name in 1836, and it soon became a significant stagecoach stop from Belvidere to "Peketonikia," which became Macktown, an early settlement in Winnebago County. The only landmark left from Rollinsville is a stone home located on McKinley Street south

Sign showing the location of the Shattuck homestead, which has the original beams. *Photo by author.*

of Woodstock Road. Even today, the home has a significant location near Woodstock Road and Illinois Route 76. The home was built by Stephen Mack and his wife, the Indian princess Hononegah. Mack is famous for settling Macktown, located where the Rock River meets the Pecatonica River.

Scotch Grove, another significant community, was established in 1836 in western central Boone County, and its story begins in Scotland with John Greenlee. Greenlee, a mason, had to escape his native land by wearing women's clothing and made his way to America, where he first landed in Ottawa. There he worked on the Illinois–Mississippi Canal. Greenlee, John Armour and two others ventured north in 1836 and claimed land in Boone County, where they built a fourteen- by fourteen-foot cabin near the site of "an Indian wigwam built of poles."

By the spring of 1837, Greenlee's six children had joined them, and they found remnants of the Native Americans, including ashes from campfires. One story tells how the family witnessed the forced migration of those who used the land first:

> *Later they saw…Indian migrations going west, the braves mounted on their ponies, carrying their guns, and straggling along after them on foot the squaws, who carried the burdens and had the children too small to walk strapped on their backs.*

Those words were written by Daniel Harvey, who heard them from Janette O. Gregory, daughter of John Greenlee. Gregory also told the following tale of the hazards of living on the early prairie in 1837:

> *An experience of the first summer that is stamped on my memory is the prairie fire. Father and Mother were awakened about midnight by a roaring noise and on getting up and looking out; they saw, to their horror, a great fire off towards the south, driven by winds towards the house. On and on the fire came with great leaps and bounds, over the prairie, licking up the long prairie grass and brush and running up the trees as it came into the grove. It was a terrifying sight and Father fully realized there was no way of escape unless a higher power intervened. They gathered the children together and waited in agony of mind for they knew not what. When the fire was nearly upon us, seemingly from a clear sky came a deluge of rain, like a cloudburst, and extinguished the flames. Father always said "It was the Hand of God" and counted it as one of his merciful providences that the family was saved on that awful night.*

## Remarkable People and Curious Incidents

The Shattuck homestead barn also has the original beams. This is the barn where the traveler died. *Photo by author.*

The early Scotch settlers in that area also reported traces of General Scott's march through Boone County. They reported tracks and ruts made by wagons, and artillery pieces were visible for a long time.

In a pattern that has been followed through the decades and centuries, the first to arrive would send signals to friends and relatives, who would, in turn, follow the pioneers. Such is the story of the Daniel Bliss and Walt Rice families and Candice Case, seven travelers who left their homes in Collinsville, Connecticut, in 1838. Bliss came to Boone County with his wife and two children; Rice came with his wife. The first part of their trek was a trip on the Erie Canal and the Great Lakes to Chicago, a journey that cost $58.75 for all seven travelers.

Once in Chicago, they hired three drivers and three "span" of horses to take them and their belongings to Boone County. The trip was rugged. Many times, after becoming stuck in mud, they had to unload all of their belongings, add extra horses to pull the rigs out of trouble, reload and continue to the next roadblock. More than once, they got lost on the prairie as they sloshed through the wetlands and across rivers and streams. They were seeking a cabin owned by Mrs. Rice, Candace Case's cousin. When they finally arrived one night in the early summer, it was a surprise. The travelers were met by Mrs. Rice, who held a saucer of grease with a rag for a wick as the only light at the cabin door. One of the newcomers, surprised by the sight of woman, exclaimed, "It is the Garden of Eden, and there's old Adam himself."

There was no food for the travelers other than some Indian corn that was ground into cornmeal by a hand-turned coffee grinder. The next day, a friend was sent to a neighbor for food, returning only with potatoes, salt pork and some white flour. The feast for their arrival consisted of pork cooked in a tin oven, called a baker, over the hearth in the cabin. They weren't the only new arrivals. But July of that year, seventeen people lived in that one-room, fourteen-square-foot cabin, but "true hospitality prevailed."

Alvah and Catherine Cady are thought to be the first permanent white settlers in Manchester Township, Boone County's northwesternmost township. Like the story of the Blisses, Rices and Case, the Cadys had an eventful trip from their home in Steuben County, New York, in November 1836. The Cadys and their five children joined other families from New York in a move west. After taking the Erie Canal to Buffalo, they boarded the steamer *Pennsylvania* to Chicago. Once arriving in Chicago, they found they had to pay a landing fee because there was no public landing place available to them. The cost to unload their goods was twenty-five cents for every one hundred pounds.

After the family crossed the Chicago River via a rope ferry, they contracted for a teamster to take them to Downer's Grove for twenty dollars. The family remained there while Alvah and his brother walked to the Rock River, headed north to Roscoe, then headed west and stayed for a while with General Brown. It was a fortuitous visit because they returned for the family with an ox team and wagon that they had borrowed from Brown. They headed west again, fording streams as they went, including the Des Plaines and Fox Rivers, and stopped in St. Charles, where Alvah paid one dollar for one hundred friction matches, which he had never seen. However, only about half were good.

The family kept moving west until they got to the Kite River near Rochelle, where they became stuck in the mud. They were stranded on the prairie, kept awake all night by the howls of wolves. They were hoping to cross the Kishwaukee River, but the bridge had not been completed, so they forded the waterway. The only thing that saved them from toppling their wagon into the river was Catherine blocking the wheels. They made it to Beaver Creek the next day and then on to Brown's claim.

# Remarkable People and Curious Incidents

Although it took some time for Cady to stake his claim in Boone County, once he did the family set to work, building a cabin in a day, with Brown furnishing the boards for the floor, roof and beds from a nearby gristmill. This wasn't the last long trek for Alvah. In the winter of 1837–38, he walked to Southport, known now as Kenosha, Wisconsin, a distance of sixty-five miles in one day, to buy leather for shoes for his children. He returned home two days later. Catherine Cady set up a school in the family log cabin, teaching her children along with Brown's. During the first winter, Alvah worked for wages to support his family. At the same time, he cut and split enough wood to fence ten acres.

While many pioneers were staking claims on the land, which would become a great source of agricultural production, others aimed for settlements, including the city that would be named for its beautiful view.

# The Legend of
# Big Thunder

It is difficult to imagine the life and hardships that the earliest residents of Boone County endured. However, it is also romantic to envision what it would have been like to be the first pioneers to live off the land. One such man was Jared B. Gould. He was born in a log cabin in Rensselaer County, New York, on May 26, 1820, and his family moved twice to new locations in New York before his father, Ira Gould, headed west to Illinois in 1836. When Ira Gould first stepped onto our county's soil, it was still owned by the government, and land surveys had not yet been completed. He staked a claim in southeastern Boone County, in Spring Township. After he and his son, Ransom, built a log cabin, Ira returned to New York State on horseback in the early winter. All but one of the Gould family arrived the following spring after a three-week journey. Jared, seventeen, didn't make the trip with the family because he was ill. When he was well enough, he sailed on Lake Erie to Toledo and then took off on foot for Chicago. After a time, he caught up with his family.

The Boone County Jared first saw in Spring Township was a wild prairie, but one with promise because of the many springs that gave the township its name. The Goulds lived off the land, and game was in abundance at that time, but their diet did not include much bread. Once, the family bought a barrel of flour for $12, and when they opened it, they found that the flour had gotten wet. What was left had dried and was forged into a solid mass that could be rolled around on the ground like a ball. Jared worked the land with his father for two years and then struck out on his own, first working in a lead smelting operation in Mineral Point, Wisconsin, and then

# Boone County Originals

*Above*: A close-up photo of the head of the statue of the Native American meant to represent Big Thunder. *Photo by author.*

*Left*: A full-body shot of the statue of the Native American. The actual title of the sculpture by Glenna Goodacre is *He Is, They Are*. It is meant to depict the forced removal of Native Americans from their lands, such as Boone County. This is why the figure is looking down and has his hands tied behind his back. *Photo by author.*

## Remarkable People and Curious Incidents

cutting wood at the headwaters of the Pecatonica River. After six months, he returned with $100 in silver from his earnings, which he used to buy eighty acres of government land in two sections of Spring Township.

Besides being a pioneer with an independent streak, Jared Gould was a perceptive entrepreneur. He married Charlotte Blackford in October 1845, but instead of working his land, he began to make shingles and roof buildings for the new settlers. He was successful at that and eventually increased his land ownership up to four hundred acres of prime agricultural soil. Jared and Charlotte raised six children, although they lost four in infancy, and eventually were able to buy seven acres of Kishwaukee riverfront land in Belvidere in 1881 on which they retired.

Boone County was built on the shoulders of men like Jared Gould, as well as Simon P. Doty, Dr. Daniel Whitney, Dr. Josiah Goodhue and Ebenezer Peck, who came to Belvidere shortly after John Towner. In August 1835, these four men joined Nathanial Crosby and, with $10,000, organized the Belvidere Company to build grist- and sawmills. By the next year, using lumber cut and hewn by hand, they had built the first sawmill, the Crosby Mill, on the rapidly flowing Kishwaukee. A second mill was completed in 1837 for grinding grain. Eventually, the county would have twelve mills, one of which was built in 1845 for $12,000 and still stands today.

The Baltic Mill ceased to operate in 1918 and became part of Belvidere Park. In the 1990s, it was renovated. Today, it is a popular site for meetings and perhaps the most photographed landmark in the county. Every fall and

Late nineteenth-century photo of the Baltic Mill. *Courtesy of the Boone County Historical Museum.*

The Baltic Mill in Belvidere Park on an early spring day. Originally built in 1837, it was renovated in the 1990s and is a popular place for meetings and concerts. *Photo by author.*

Simon's drawing of Baltic Mill. *Courtesy Gary Simon.*

spring, dozens of high school students use the mill as a scenic background for homecoming and prom pictures.

Simon P. Doty, the second child of Solomon and Hannah Shaw Doty, could trace his ancestry to 1620, when his great-great-great-grandfather Edward Doty arrived on the *Mayflower*. The Doty family were respected members of the upper class in England, with lineage dating back to the Norman Conquest. However, Norman law at the time dictated that the oldest son received the family inheritance. As the second son, Edward Doty was obliged to serve a seven-year apprenticeship, which he entered with Stephen Hopkins. Among the signers of the Mayflower Compact on November 21, 1620, are Stephen Hopkins, listed as the fourteenth witness after William Bradford (second) and Myles Standish (sixth), and Edward Doty (fortieth). Edward Leister, number forty-one, was an

Big Thunder Park in Belvidere, site of Chief Big Thunder's grave. *Photo by author.*

apprentice, too. Neither Doty son was known for his strict puritanical ways because they fought a duel with swords and daggers. One injured a thigh; the other, a hand. Each had to serve a punishment of having his head and feet tied together for a day without food or water.

Such are the roots of one of Boone County's most celebrated and interesting original settlers. Born Simon Potter Doty in New York, he changed his middle name to Phineas while in Boone County. His first endeavor was as a sailor along the East Coast, and he eventually married Elizabeth Brewster. In the summer of 1835, he and Dr. Daniel Whitney were headed west out of Chicago. They hired a man to drive them, but when the driver got drunk in Elgin, the two men walked the remaining distance. Upon arrival in August 1835, they saw the John Towner family camped on the south bank of the Kishwaukee River. In short order, they pooled their resources with Dr. Josiah Goodhue, Ebenezer Peck and Nathaniel Crosby to establish a permanent settlement.

Another view of the Indian statue meant to represent Big Thunder. *Photo by author.*

# Remarkable People and Curious Incidents

Ebenezer Peck is credited with naming that settlement Belvidere. He suggested that the name of the new settlement reflect the surrounding flowering prairies and attractive waterways. So he took the Latin words *belle ve dere* and named the place Belvidere.

Doty continued to develop the new community. He and Crosby laid out the four corners of North State Street and Lincoln Avenue (then known as Mechanic Street) with an iron carpenter's square. Doty then built a twenty-four- by eighteen-foot frame house on the north bank of the river. The building boom continued as Whitney put up a tavern at the southwest corner of State and Lincoln and hired Doty to be the manager. Those two buildings were among the first frame buildings in county history.

Whitney picked the perfect location for his tavern, for it was on the new stagecoach route. The Frink and Walker stage line came into Belvidere via Lawrenceville Road, crossed the Kishwaukee and followed its southern bend along the river before turning west. The bend along the river became Lincoln Avenue, and the stage turned to the north onto State Street. The tavern on the corner grew to include a dining room and room for guests. At one end were a bar and storeroom that eventually became Asher Jenner's watch shop. Doty and Goodhue were granted the

Mid-nineteenth-century drawing of Simon P. Doty. *Courtesy of the Boone County Historical Museum.*

county's first liquor license on June 6, 1837, for a fee of five dollars. The court regulated the hotel prices in September 1837 as follows:

37½ cents for a meal
12½ cents for a night's lodging
18¾ cents "for horse to hay"
50 cents for a peck of oats
6 cents for a drink of liquor

The Belvidere stop on the stage route from Chicago to Galena was a busy one. Horses were changed here, and the passengers often had a wait of thirty minutes to an hour or were delayed for other reasons. It was a time for a pleasant diversion, and what better one than to see a genuine Indian at his final resting place? Most of the travelers had never seen such a sight, and they had the time, so why not take the short walk up the hill to the place where Big Thunder's body lay?

Much has been written about Big Thunder, and most of the stories have the same narrative. He was said to have been a Potawatomi Indian chief who abhorred the arrival of the Europeans. Upon his death, he requested that his body be placed in a sitting position—facing north because that is the direction from which the spirits of Native American ancestors would come and impose their wrath on the encroaching white men, and the Indians would regain their lost land. This is a familiar legend in Native American lore and was probably commonly known in the early nineteenth century. Although Big Thunder was hopeful of a mighty change in fortune, he was also pragmatic and wanted to help those he left behind. He instructed his people to place him in an enclosure of split logs, six feet long, surrounded by his favorite weapons. He was to be fully clothed, and his pockets were to be stuffed with items, including tobacco. The idea was that as travelers came upon his remains, they would snatch a plug of tobacco for their trip and, upon returning, replace the tobacco for future travelers.

However, as more travelers and visitors began to arrive, they did what people do to this day: they carved their names into logs, or whatever was available, and took a souvenir. Soon, visitors began to take more than they left. Not only were Big Thunder's clothes taken but also parts of his body. As pieces were being spirited away, it was said that Dr. Josiah Goodhue, one of Belvidere's original settlers, took his head for safekeeping. There is one story that he hung it in his home and that its dangling appearance startled

# Remarkable People and Curious Incidents

Local artist Troy Yunk's drawing of the burial ground of Chief Big Thunder. *Courtesy Troy Yunk.*

a visitor. The skull was eventually taken to Chicago for further study by doctors there.

As more of the Indian's bones began to disappear, local folks would collect dried bones of hogs and other animals and toss them into Big Thunder's burial area. And travelers would scoop them up, believing they had the real thing. Early histories of the county speculate that many museums in the country at that time displayed Big Thunder's bones.

There is little doubt that there was a burial site a short distance from the Belvidere House. However, it is unlikely that it actually was the burial site of an Indian chief. In all likelihood, it was a creation of Simon P. Doty.

A search of comprehensive histories of Native Americans does not list any chief who went by Big Thunder. There are no dates of his birth and death. There is no mention of Big Thunder in the pre–Black Hawk War history of Boone County, and his name shows up only after the arrival of Doty and others. However, that doesn't mean that he couldn't have existed, and that alone is enough for the legend of Big Thunder to remain a part of local history.

During the time that Doty ran the Belvidere House, he probably created the legend of Big Thunder to get people who stopped at the hotel to stay and spend some money. In his later years, Doty was described as being known for telling pioneer and Indian stories. And he liked to laugh and tell jokes. One of those gags may have been the Big Thunder legend.

If Doty did create Big Thunder, then he may have believed his own story to be true, for when he was in his eighties, he told a story about a plug of tobacco. Doty and Erastus Nixon, another original settler, were cutting and trimming wood when Doty had a craving for tobacco. As they worked, Nixon asked Doty for a bit of chew, and Doty said he had none. One of the traditions about Big Thunder's grave site was that when Indians would pass it, they would toss plugs onto the chief's lap. Doty knew this, and when he happened to pass by the grave site, he grabbed enough tobacco for a chew and hid it from Nixon. Later, as the two worked, Doty spit out a wad and it landed on a wood chip. Nixon eyed the chip and said, "Doty, you have tobacco!" Doty admitted that he did but pointed out that he hadn't had it when Nixon first asked him. They laughed about the incident then and years later, when Doty continued to tell the story.

Over the years, Doty became a respected citizen. He was elected the county's first sheriff in 1837, and two years later, the north room of his home was designated as the first jail. He was given a contract of $250 for the use of his home until a permanent jail could be constructed. In 1840, when a flood washed out the first bridge over the Kishwaukee River, Doty ran a ferry until a new bridge could be built. Doty was elected to Boone County's first state legislature and remained a key citizen until his death on November 1, 1885, at the age of eighty-seven.

Part of Doty's obituary in the newspaper read:

> *Mr. Doty was a remarkable man in many respects. His greatest victory was over his own self. Many years ago, he drank to such an excess that the danger was apparent to him and others. With a firm resolve, he stopped at once and from a hard drinker became a teetotaler of the strictest sort. When he was eighty years of age, he gave a reception. He was then straight and active and full of life and joviality, keeping the company in a roar with his stories of the early settlement.*

In the years after the county was settled, there began some tugging and pulling of boundaries as allegiances were established with one geographic area or another. Some of these succeeded, others did not. One boundary decision is not well known, and had it succeeded, Boone County would have been one of the southernmost counties in Wisconsin. The dispute reaches back to the

# Remarkable People and Curious Incidents

Northwest Ordinance of 1787, which carved out territory west of the original colonies where as many as five states could be established, all of which were to be free of slavery. The states were Ohio, Michigan, Indiana, Illinois and Wisconsin.

The original map of the territories has some familiar boundaries. Ohio changed the least, save for the northwestern stretch that includes Toledo. Michigan was smaller, Wisconsin larger and Illinois and Indiana shared a common northern boundary. These territories could achieve statehood when each had at least sixty thousand residents. The ordinance indicated that when Illinois became a state, its northern border would be formed from the southernmost bend of Lake Michigan to the Mississippi River. However, a visionary named Nathanial Pope looked at the projected state map and realized that Illinois' access to Lake Michigan would be minimal. Realizing the economic advantage of having access to Lake Michigan—and eventually, the world—Pope, the first territorial secretary of Illinois, successfully amended the original statehood bill to move the northern boundary of Illinois sixty-one miles to the north. "It was a matter of state pride having a harbor on Lake Michigan," said Royal Brunson Way of Beloit College in his 1926 book, *The Rock River Valley*.

When Illinois became a state in 1818, the line that Pope promoted became the state's northern boundary. In an address to the Chicago Historical Society on May 19, 1904, William Radebaugh stated that Pope's accomplishment "was one of the most decisive events in Illinois history, and an event of much significance for the nation at large." In an article in the *Rockford Register Star*, the late U.S. senator Paul Simon said, "No one knows how different things would have been if the boundary was changed." One thing that would be different was that Boone County would be one of Wisconsin's southernmost counties instead of one of Illinois' northernmost. And that led to the boundary dispute, also called the "Cheddar Curtain."

After the Black Hawk War of 1832, Wisconsin began to grow in population, and its territorial leaders saw that the northern tier of counties in Illinois included even more residents, numbers that would help it move closer to sixty thousand residents and statehood. In his address to the Chicago Historical Society, Radebaugh stated that Wisconsin desired to regain its original land taken in the border adjustment. A meeting in November 1840 was held in Madison to discuss the "necessary and proper…adjustment of the southern boundary and admission into the Union of a State of Wisconsin on an equal footing with the original states in all respects whatever." Earlier that year, residents in the northern tier of counties were asked about their "sentiments" regarding the matter, and meetings were held in Jo Daviess, Stephenson, Boone, Carroll, Ogle, Whiteside, Winnebago, Rock Island and McHenry Counties to discuss the matter and appoint delegates to a July 6, 1840 meeting in Rockford. At that meeting, delegates discussed whether the Ordinance of 1787 had been violated and, knowing they were citizens of Illinois, whether action should be taken as soon as possible to determine where they "legally and rightfully belonged." The centers of the secession movement were Rockford and Galena, and at one point, each settlement was asked if it would consider sending a delegate to the next statehood convention in Wisconsin.

Wisconsin territorial governor Judge J.D. Doty was a fervent supporter of returning these counties to Wisconsin. In a message to the territorial legislature, he said that "8,500 acres have been wrongfully taken from Wisconsin and should be restored." On the Illinois side, there was great support in these northern counties for joining the neighbor to the north. As Illinois became populated, growing from 55,162 in 1820 to 269,974 in 1835, most of the migration came from the southeast and northeast. The south and central parts of Illinois were settled by people from Kentucky, Tennessee and Virginia. The northern part of the state was populated by people from New England, New York and other eastern states who began to arrive in great numbers via the Erie Canal and the Great Lakes. But these settlers mostly came after the Black Hawk War. By then, the other parts of the state had already been carved up and platted out. While those who lived downstate could not hold slaves by law, they generally supported slavery. The northerners were mostly opposed to slavery, and they were known to call their southern neighbors "crackers."

In addition to having little in common with these "crackers," those in the north believed they were being taxed unfairly by the state. In order to provide necessary services for the settled portions of the state, Illinois began to build roads and canals. The cost of these projects reached $1,528,000 by 1842, and the people of the north were expected to pay their share. Believing they had nothing to do with this debt, they felt bullied. "And, when an opportunity of escape is given, it is quite natural for the weaker party to seek to get away," Radebaugh said. So the people of northern Illinois were the first to want to escape to Wisconsin.

Wisconsin had another reason to take a chunk of Illinois for itself. When Ohio gained the port of Toledo and access to the Maumee River from Michigan, Michigan's compensation was the western Upper Peninsula, which was part of Wisconsin. Having lost land to Illinois and Michigan,

# Remarkable People and Curious Incidents

Wisconsin believed that northern Illinois rightfully belonged to it. And lobbying for that addition picked up steam in Illinois.

The *Chicago American* reported in its March 7, 1840 edition, "There is so little sympathy between the people of this region and those of the southern and middle portion of the State that I apprehend they will mutually shake hands and part without much grief on either side." On March 25, 1840, a letter to the *Chicago American* from a resident of Pecatonica in Winnebago County wrote, "We are firmly convinced that we are justly part of Wisconsin by a law older than our revered federal constitution." Wisconsin sweetened the pot by offering incentives, including the naming of a Chicago resident as senator and selecting Galena as the territorial capital.

Beginning in January 1842, voters in several counties in the disputed territory were asked if they wanted to become part of Wisconsin. The results were stunning; they were near unanimous. In Stephenson County, the vote to join Wisconsin was approved 570 to 1. In Winnebago County, the vote was 971 to 6. In Boone County, it was 455 to 11. With this tremendous support, Governor Doty wrote a letter to Illinois governor Thomas Carlin, stating that Illinois' jurisdiction over the disputed area was "accidental and temporary." Carlin, believing his state was not about to give up land to which it was entitled, simply ignored the letter. Doty wrote three more, and Carlin ignored those as well. In time, the matter quietly faded away.

The state began to spend more money in the region, including on improvements of the Rock River. Construction began on the railroad from Chicago to Galena. And Thomas Ford was elected governor in 1842. Ford had been a judge in northern Illinois from 1835 to 1841, and people believed he had the best interests of the area in mind. The dispute about the "Cheddar Curtain," as described by Michael D. Sublett and Frederick H. Walk in the Illinois Periodicals Online Project, ended for good in 1848, when Wisconsin became a state.

There is a postscript to this story, one that affected history. Some believe that the vote in the northern tier counties helped to elect the Republican Party ticket in 1856. That secured the party for the state and made possible the election of Abraham Lincoln as president in 1860.

# The Railroad Arrives

In 1836, a charter was issued by the state legislature in Springfield for the Galena and Chicago Union Railroad, the first railroad to be built west of Chicago. William Ogden of Chicago spearheaded the drive to build this railroad by selling stock in the company. The line was needed to provide a rail link between the growing city of Chicago and the lead mining center of Galena in northwestern Illinois.

Ogden sold stock to farmers and others in the area who would benefit by having their crops and products shipped to Chicago and on to larger markets. According to the *Rockford Register-Gazette* of May 31, 1907, on November 28, 1845, a meeting was held in Rockford at which it was determined that the counties interested in having a railroad would send delegates to a conference in January 1846. At the same meeting, those attending related that the railroad organizers would make open subscription books available in Rockford and Galena, as well as in the settlements through which the railroad was to pass. One of those settlements was Belvidere, and among those "subscribing" were Simon Doty, Allen Fuller, William Holt Gilman, Stephen Hurlbut and Seth Whitman. Doty pledged $1,000, while the largest subscription was $2,000 from Gilman. Over time, Ogden was able to raise more than $350,000, allowing the railroad to purchase a third-hand locomotive, the Pioneer, along with three passenger cars and thirteen freight cars on October 10, 1848.

Construction began in 1848, and by October of that year, the tracks had reached Oak Park, west of Chicago. The first shipment on the new line was wheat from Belvidere. The line reached West Chicago in the spring of

*Left*: Drawing of the Pioneer, the first train engine that came through Boone County. *Courtesy of the Boone County Historical Museum.*

*Below*: Stone monument showing the location of Ames Tavern outside of Garden Prairie. *Photo by author.*

1849 and Elgin in January 1850. Eventually, the railroad reached Marengo. The locomotives of the time needed regular supplies of wood and water every eight to ten miles, and that put the next stop near the settlement of Amesville. To most, the idea of a new transportation method was exciting.

## Remarkable People and Curious Incidents

But it wasn't exciting to George Ames, son of William Ames. William Ames was one of the original settlers in Bonus Township. He arrived in 1836 and soon built a tavern in a double log cabin on the Frink and Walker Chicago–Galena stagecoach trail. Those who followed him had to endure a terrible winter in 1837, followed by a dry summer and an early frost. Most farmers had no crops to bring to Chicago to buy groceries, so they were forced to live on what they had, such as bean soup, turnips, salt pork, cornmeal, potatoes and milk.

In those days, teamsters needed four to six days to bring goods from Amesville to Chicago. Cows and pigs were herded to market. Corn and oats were never shipped because the prices were thought to be too low. Seeing the need for a middleman, and filling that need in the small community, Ames opened a general store at his tavern and allowed settlers to trade their corn and potatoes for sugar, molasses and salt. Business was so good that he built a larger tavern. When William Ames died in 1840, he left the prosperous business to his son, George.

Stone monument of Ames Tavern with the building in the background. *Photo by author.*

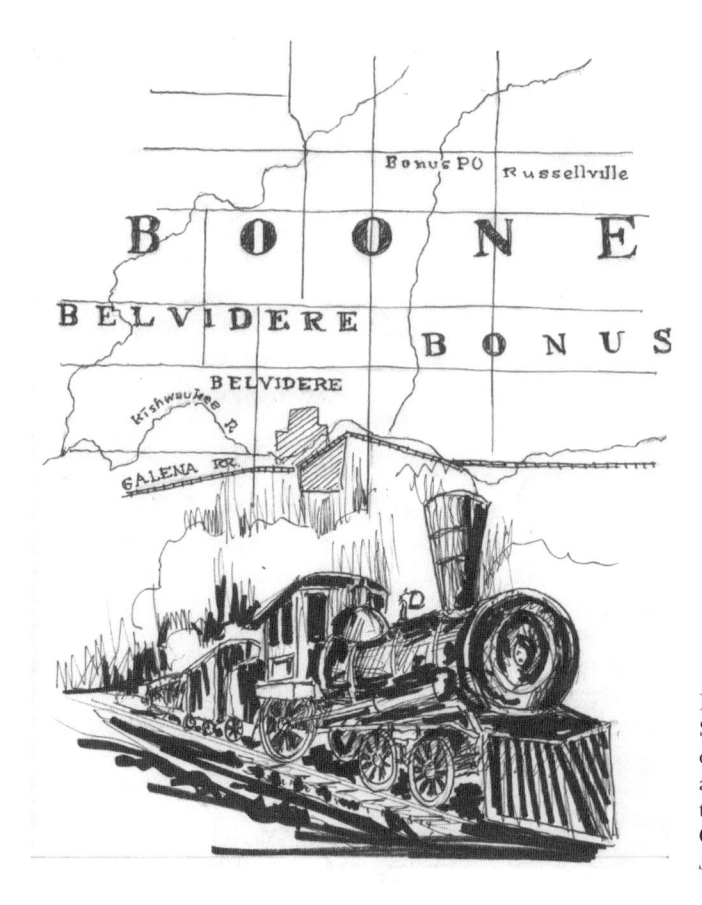

Local artist Kit Scheidenhelm's drawing of the arrival of the train in Boone County. *Courtesy Kit Scheidenhelm.*

When the first train ran between Chicago and Elgin in 1850, the forty-two-mile distance was covered in three hours. Compared to the early days, when it took days to bridge such distances, the railroad seemed like a great advantage. But George Ames believed the railroad was going to ruin his business. Although the family land was on the projected right of way, he flatly refused to sell to the railroad. In fact, he built a house directly in the railroad's path and rented it to a "hot-headed Irish family," according to local history. When the railroad came through, the home Ames built on the right of way was moved off to the side.

Ames also refused the offer to become the depot agent, insisting on running the tavern. In 1851, a railroad station was built one and a quarter miles east of Ames Tavern. The stagecoach still serviced the tavern, in part because the railroad schedule was not always reliable. Many travelers on the stage line and others passing through on the State Road were on their way to the

# Remarkable People and Curious Incidents

Ames Tavern in Garden Prairie on the original Frink and Walker stagecoach line from Chicago to Galena. *Photo by author.*

California gold fields. Wagons heading west boasted "California or Bust," while many made the return trip with the slogan "Busted by Thunder." Stagecoach service ended in 1853, and by 1860, business at the tavern had busted, too, and it closed.

A new community grew up around the railroad station built east of Ames Tavern. It was identified only by number until a woman stepped off a Galena and Chicago car and was impressed by the prairie landscape. "How beautiful it is," she said. "It looks like a garden on the prairie." From that point on, the community has been known as Garden Prairie.

The next stop on the Galena and Chicago line was Belvidere, and plans had been made for a railroad bridge in Belvidere, which was growing quite rapidly, mostly on the north side of the Kishwaukee River. By 1851, the north side of Belvidere was boasting "long rows of teams [that] were ranged along the walks, the stores were full, the three hotels having all the business they could provide for," according to the *Belvidere Standard*. The locals were excited about the new line coming and were said to have "railroad on the brain."

William Holt Gilman, an original subscriber of the Galena and Chicago Union Railroad, had "railroad on the brain," too. Only he had a different idea. He owned land on the south side of the Kishwaukee River, an area that the newspaper described as having "no existence. We think a scattering house or two was visible on the prairie," and there was "no use for a town over there, as nobody could get to it." One of the least inhabitable areas along the river was known as the flats. Gilman realized that his land would be worthless if the railroad followed its original course and established a depot on the other side of the river. So he informed the railroad that he would give it right of way—that is, donate his land to the railroad—if it would be built on the south side of the river. The railroad, seeing a bargain, did just that. As a result, the depot was built on the south side, between Main Street and Whitney Boulevard, and Belvidere's downtown grew up around it, instead of on the other side of the river.

Gilman's offer changed the original urban plan for Belvidere. Most of its early settlers were from New York and New England, and they planned the city to have a New England–style city center with a public square surrounded by significant businesses and governmental offices. And that is how Belvidere was originally laid out. But Gilman knew that the location of the railroad depot would immediately become an economic engine, as businesses that sold cigars and general goods, as well as hotels and barbershops, would want to locate near where passengers were coming and going. So downtown Belvidere grew around the rerouted railroad line. The town square still exists, with the Boone County Courthouse and Public Safety Building on one side. But the other three sides are lined with homes, an arrangement that helps to explain why the county seat of government is located several blocks north of downtown Belvidere.

The railroad's location also caused the demise of the village of Newburg. As described in chapter two, Newburg was a thriving settlement on the western edge of the county on the Kishwaukee River. Its potential for growth rivaled Belvidere for several years, until Gilman's gift caused the railroad line to run on the south side of the Kishwaukee. Newburg was located on the north side of the Kishwaukee, so when the line was built, Newburg had no access. For many years, it was largely forgotten, but it lives today in the names of two roads: Newburg Road and Distillery Road, named for the distillery once located in the village. Newburg's demise did have a positive impact on another nearby community. Because the railroad was located on the south side of the Kishwaukee River, the village of Cherry Valley in Winnebago County was established along the line.

# Remarkable People and Curious Incidents

Sign showing the former location of Newburg Village. *Photo by author.*

The Galena and Chicago line eventually became the Chicago and North Western Railroad. The line that crossed Boone County from east to west was known as the Galena Division. In 1853, the Madison Branch of the railroad, originally known as the Beloit Branch, was completed between Belvidere and Beloit and included a station in Caledonia. Caledonia can trace its name to early immigrants who came from Aberdeen, Scotland. The name can be traced to Gavin Ralston, who took it from one of the poetic names for Scotland. Caledonia became an important railroad link after the Kenosha Division line was laid from Kenosha to Rockford in 1857. This line was known as the K.D. line. In Boone County, it passed through Capron, Poplar Grove, Caledonia junction and Argyle before crossing into Winnebago County.

Because it was served by two railroad lines, one of Caledonia's most significant businesses became the Chamberlain Hotel. Originally built by William Gilkerson and R.H. Emerson, it became the property of Catherine Chamberlain in December 1878.

The Chicago, Madison and Northern Railroad, which would become the Illinois Central, came to southern Boone County in 1886, and one of its stops was in Irene. It was common then for stations to be located about ten miles apart because that was the range of a farmer's horse. At one time, ten passenger trains a day passed through, and a milk train left for Chicago at 7:00 a.m. every day and returned at 4:00 p.m. In 1901, a passenger train and a freight train collided head-on at the River Road curve, causing many deaths.

Irene was named for an eight-year-old daughter of the Maguire family, who gave the railroad land for a station. It once had two general stores, a blacksmith shop, a barbershop and a post office. One practical joke from the early twentieth century from Irene nearly backfired. George Banks set on fire a patch of tar that had been spilled when a road was built adjacent to the railroad. The fire was so large that it nearly burned down the town and warped a switch track so badly that people could walk under the rails. Irene was such an important station on the Illinois Central line that bags bound for Dubuque, Iowa, were marked "Chicago-Irene-Dubuque." The railroad ran from 1888 until February 21, 1964, and at one time, three railroad agents manned the station full time. As roads improved, as did the efficiency of cars and trucks, railroads no longer needed closely located stations, and soon they didn't need them at all.

The arrival of the railroad and its effect on local history and geography cannot be overlooked. By 1864, there were an estimated 860 miles of track in Boone County, and they provided an economic boost to the manufacturing engine that continues to thrive here. Several presidents made whistle-stops in Belvidere, including President Herbert Hoover.

Even today, the railroad has an impact. One of the biggest recent stories in local news was the announcement by Illinois governor Pat Quinn that the new Amtrak line will stop in Belvidere. And maybe, when the first train pulls into town, there will be the same kind of reaction that took place in December 1851. One schoolboy was so excited when he heard the whistle that he jumped out of the classroom window to see the first train arrive. His teacher chased him and arrived just in time to see that first train, too.

President Herbert Hoover on a whistle-stop tour in Belvidere. *Courtesy of the Boone County Historical Museum.*

# "I Was a Soldier!"

Boone County made a remarkable contribution to the Union cause during the Civil War. The Ninety-fifth Regiment of Illinois Infantry Volunteers included men from Boone and McHenry Counties who fought major battles, including the Vicksburg, Mississippi Campaign and Siege; the Red River Expedition into Louisiana; the Atlanta Campaign; and the siege and capture of Mobile, Alabama. The Ninety-fifth also took part in the search for Confederate general Nathan Bedford Forrest and the repulse of General John Bell Hood at Nashville, Tennessee. In the course of the rebellion, the soldiers traveled by rail and steamboat and on foot, logging about 9,960 miles.

Also, Belvidere was able to boast that it was the hometown of two Union officers: Adjutant General Allen C. Fuller and General Stephen Hurlbut. Each made notable contributions during and after the war. And one of the most controversial individuals from the war—a true original—had a Boone County connection. The story of Albert Cashier, a private in Company G of the Ninety-fifth, is one of endurance and heroism, made even more remarkable when it became known years later that Albert Cashier was really a woman, Jennie Hodgers.

Sources differ as to how many women dressed as men and fought in the Civil War. Among the well-documented occurrences is the story of Jennie Hodgers, who was born in Clogher Head Parish, near Belfast, Ireland, on December 25, 1843, to Denis and Catherine Hodgers. She had three sisters and two brothers (one her twin), and would tend to the sheep on her father's farm with her brothers. Because the chores and the work on the farm were

Scheidenhelm's drawing of the county's Civil War history. *Courtesy Kit Scheidenhelm.*

hard, it was logical that she wore her brothers' clothes. When the family immigrated to the United States in the early 1860s, she continued the habit of wearing her twin brother's clothes. After the family suffered the tragic deaths of Catherine, one of Jennie's three sisters, and her twin brother, Denis, Jennie's older brother deserted her.

To this day, there is no clear information that tells how Jennie wound up in Belvidere, but she enlisted in Company G of the Ninety-fifth Illinois Infantry Volunteers on August 3, 1862, one of the last to enlist in the company. At that time, the army didn't give complete physicals, and the fact that Hodgers was apparently healthy was enough for Union army officials.

On or about that date, Jennie Hodgers ceased to exist; she was replaced by Albert D.J. Cashier. At five feet, three inches tall and 110 pounds, Albert was the shortest soldier in the company and the regiment. He was described as having fair skin, blue eyes and auburn-colored hair. After training at

# Remarkable People and Curious Incidents

Civil War solider Albert Cashier (Jennie Hodgers) is on the right. *Courtesy of the Boone County Historical Museum.*

Camp Fuller in Rockford, the Ninety-fifth was sent to Jackson, Mississippi, to become attached to General Ulysses Grant's Army of the Tennessee. The Ninety-fifth saw action in more than forty battles and skirmishes, but perhaps none was as significant as the Siege of Vicksburg, Mississippi. Situated on a bluff overlooking the Mississippi River, Vicksburg was a key objective for Union forces, for whoever controlled the town and the bluff controlled the mighty Mississippi.

In preparation for the Siege of Vicksburg, the Ninety-fifth steamed from Memphis to Milliken's Bend on January 26, 1863, as Grant tried to complete an "end run" around Vicksburg. During a march along the river to Grand Gulf, the unit met Confederate resistance. Because he was small and apparently fearless, Cashier was often chosen for foraging and skirmish duty. In one of those skirmishes, he was reportedly captured by Confederate soldiers, but somehow he grabbed a weapon from a guard, knocked the soldier down and high-tailed it back to the Union lines.

Another report describes Cashier as an equal to his comrades in arms. "He was the equal to any in this company," wrote Gerhard P. Clausius. "In spite of his lack of height and brawn, he was able to withstand…the problems of an infantryman as well as his comrades who were bigger and brawnier."

In a letter printed by a Belvidere newspaper about 1913, former lieutenant Charles W. Ives, Cashier's officer, told that Company G was in a firefight near Fort Hill at Vicksburg on May 19, 1864. The Union forces were able to drive the Confederates from their guns and into hiding places when Cashier jumped onto a fallen tree and yelled at them, "Why don't you get up, you darned Rebs, where we can see you?" Just as Ives ordered Cashier down, a hail of bullets came crashing toward Cashier, but he was not hit.

During the Siege of Vicksburg, Cashier became ill with chronic diarrhea and reported to the regimental hospital. Either the illness was not very serious or Cashier had a convincing story because he was treated and released as an outpatient and was not admitted, a situation that may have led to the discovery of his true gender.

Cashier was attached to Company G until he was mustered out on August 17, 1865, after three years and twelve days of service. During his later years, he planned to go into business in Belvidere with Samuel Pepper. Letters home from Pepper include many comments about pants and other clothing that they hoped to sell. Cashier returned to Boone County to work at odd jobs and then left in 1869 for Saunemin, Illinois, where he worked for a farmer, Joshua Chesebro. There, he built a one-room home and worked as a farmhand and gardener; he also had jobs like lighting the streetlamps and ringing the church bells. Cashier was eccentric, sometimes offering friends food and then telling them it was poisoned "to fool the rats." He enjoyed being around children, but they also turned on him. Because of his small size, they teased him about his military experience and called him "Drummer Boy." He would yell back, "I was not a drummer boy. I was a soldier!"

For the most part, he was respected for his Civil War duty. He would lead the Memorial Day parades in Saunemin, wearing his army uniform, and often attended patriotic events. He applied for a military pension in 1890, attesting that he was partially disabled because of the chronic diarrhea he experienced at Vicksburg. The claim was denied because he would not take a physical, a procedure that would have verified the claim but also would have revealed his secret. In 1907, he was granted the normal pension of twelve dollars per month.

Around the turn of the twentieth century, Cashier worked in the household of state senator Ira Lish. Cashier became ill in 1900 while in Lish's employ, and that was when his secret was first unveiled. Mrs. Patrick Lannon, a friend of Lish, sent a nurse to Cashier and was said to exclaim, "My Lord, Mrs. Lannon, he's a full-fledged woman!" Ten years later, his secret was again discovered when Senator Lish was backing his automobile out of his garage and accidentally struck Cashier below the hip. When a doctor examined his broken leg, he discovered Cashier's real sexual identity. Cashier begged the senator and the doctor not to reveal his secret, and they complied. In fact, Lish helped Cashier get into the state soldiers and sailors' home because he could not take care of himself; he convinced the hospital's administration to keep Cashier's secret as well. But two years later, when two male nurses tried to give Hodgers a bath, the secret was finally revealed. The story was a sensation as people learned that not only did Hodgers pose as a man but he was also a stowaway on a ship from Ireland.

The federal government's pension bureau became interested in the case, wondering if it was paying a pension to someone who only claimed to have been a soldier. Among those rallying behind Cashier was his former lieutenant, Ives. In his letter, Ives wrote that he recalled a case when a soldier's sex came under scrutiny, and

> *the colonel had to find the woman and send her home. In uniform, she could not be picked out; he had several of them lined up and had apples thrown to them to catch. Naturally she made a grab as if to catch it in her apron, and that was a giveaway. She was started back without delay.*

But as far as Cashier was concerned, Ives had complete confidence in her, no matter her gender. "One sure thing," he wrote. "I would never make affidavit that would deprive Cashier of a pension or anything else that is due a good soldier. She earned every bit of it. Her record would have been a credible one for any man."

Some accounts report that Cashier became stressed and increasingly uncooperative. He was declared insane and sent to the state asylum in March 1913, where he was forced to wear women's clothes. The story goes that the awkwardness of having to wear women's clothing caused him to trip on a dress, fall and break his hip. The injury was said to have led to his death on October 11, 1915, at the age of seventy-two years. But Ives's letter, dated May 21, 1913, disputes that. He says that he visited Cashier at the soldier's home, where he wore the uniform of the day, men's clothes. He added that "they all treat her with respect and seem to think her quite a noted character."

Samuel Pepper, whom Hodgers was planning on going into business with, did return to Belvidere. He wrote about 150 letters, which have been edited by local historian Frank Crawford, and in them he talks about planting little maple trees in front of his home on the 700 block of Main Street near the courthouse. The trees are still standing today.

The Ninety-fifth served with distinction and honor in the Civil War and was involved in many significant battles and skirmishes. One of the most treasured publications in Boone County history is Wales Woods's history of the Ninety-fifth. Woods, a former adjutant of the regiment, not only wrote stirring tales of bravery and honor but also of those everyday occurrences that make reading about life back then so interesting. He also noted how there was genuine concern for the soldiers. Such is the story of the tents. When the Ninety-fifth arrived in Jackson, Tennessee, in November 1862, it did not have any tents, and the ones issued were small shelters, called "dog" or "pup" tents by the troops. Colonel Thomas Humphrey, noting that other regiments were well supplied with large tents, determined that his men deserved better. He invited General McArthur to visit his camp, where he would see a demonstration of how shelters were constructed. But before the general's arrival, Humphrey sought out the tallest man in the regiment, a fellow who stood more than six feet tall. When the general inspected the tents, he saw the soldier's head and feet sticking out of the pup tent. In a matter of days, the Ninety-fifth's soldiers turned in their shelter tents for larger ones.

It seems fitting to end these descriptions of Cashier and this tall trooper by saying "that's the long and the short if it." Colonel Humphrey was killed on June 10, 1864, at the Battle of Brice's Crossroads, or Guntown, near Corinth, Mississippi. He was shot in the upper thigh while leading his men and bled to death. His body was recovered, returned to Illinois and is buried on the family farm on Cherry Valley Road south of Belvidere.

---

Stephen Hurlbut may have been the most respected individual in nineteenth-century Boone County. A lawyer, legislator, Indian fighter, Civil War general and diplomat, Hurlbut was also a trusted friend of Abraham Lincoln. Born in 1815 to a prominent family, his father was a Unitarian minister and college president from New England; his mother was from South Carolina. He spent his early days in Charleston, South Carolina, where he studied law. After passing the bar in 1837, he enlisted in the army to fight in the Seminole Indian War in Florida and eventually became a lieutenant. For some reason, he left the South in 1845 and resettled in Belvidere, where he opened a law practice and got involved in politics. He represented Boone County in 1847 at the second constitutional convention in Springfield, where he met Lincoln.

# Remarkable People and Curious Incidents

The two had a lot in common—both were born in the South and served in an Indian war and both were lawyers who were members of the Whig Party but eventually joined the Republican Party.

Despite his southern background, Hurlbut was antislavery and often spoke passionately in public on the subject, which was causing great rifts in our country's fabric. When talk of possible conflict arose in the 1850s, Hurlbut was asked to raise a volunteer military unit because of his army experience. Roll call for the Boone Rifles included twenty-one men, whose uniforms matched government standards: a blue coat with a green collar and cuffs, light blue pants with a green stripe and a cap with a green pompom. Hurlbut was named captain, and another local lawyer, Allen C. Fuller, was the first lieutenant. Mostly, the Boone Rifles took part in parades and other marching exhibitions.

Civil War hero General Stephen Hurlbut. *Courtesy of the Boone County Historical Museum.*

In 1858, Hurlbut's political friend Abraham Lincoln was running for a senate seat against Stephen Douglas. One of their historic debates was held in Freeport, and Hurlbut organized a special train to take people from Boone, Winnebago and McHenry Counties to see the event. The train contained twelve hundred people and was the longest to travel that rail line. That same year, Hurlbut was elected to the state legislature, getting support from Lincoln, who said of him, "[Hurlbut] was the ablest orator on the stump that Illinois has ever produced." Two years later, Hurlbut campaigned for his friend from Springfield and saw him elected president. Hurlbut attended Lincoln's inauguration in 1860 and, shortly after, visited his hometown, Charleston, South Carolina. The reported reason for the trip was to visit his sister, but there was another, more intriguing reason, one that could be described as espionage.

Lincoln knew that Hurlbut was born in Charleston and had friends and relatives there. So he sent his friend from Illinois on a mission to find out as much as he could about the situation there. Lincoln wanted to know if there were any Union supporters in the South and if there was a way to appeal to them. Hurlbut stayed two days with his former friends and lawyers and then returned to Washington with a report. The main point of the report was that there was nothing to appeal to.

On April 1, 1860, Lincoln made a call for troops, and on April 20, the largest town meeting in history, including people from all political parties, gathered and heard a fiery, dramatic political speech from Hurlbut. When the enlistment roll was unveiled, Hurlbut's name was the first of 115 on the list. He was made captain, and the group reported for training in Freeport. Hurlbut didn't stay with the unit long, as he was promoted to brigadier general by Lincoln and eventually took command of the Fourth Army Division of the Army of the Tennessee. Under the command of General Ulysses Grant, the Army of the Tennessee went up the Tennessee River to attack the Confederate army near Corinth, Mississippi. Grant's troops made camp at a steamboat landing on the river near a small country church called Shiloh.

The Battle of Shiloh, the first massive battle of the Civil War, took place the next day, April 7, 1862. Grant's forty thousand men were matched against Confederate general Joseph Johnston's forty-five thousand. Hurlbut fought in the Peach Orchard, where he ordered his troops to lie flat on their stomachs in a double row against Johnston's Rebels. Some accounts tell of him riding bravely in front of his troops, spurring them to challenge the Confederates. It must have been quite a scene, because on the other side, Johnston was heard shouting, "Come on! I'll lead you!" Although Johnston was killed, the Confederates did take the Peach Orchard. The Confederates claimed victory, but it was at the cost of many men. It would have been worse for the Union if Generals Buell and Wallace had not arrived with reinforcements. In scope, Shiloh was the largest battle of the war, with each side having suffered seventeen hundred men killed and eight thousand wounded.

Hurlbut's coolness under pressure was one of the bright spots for the Union. "No general handled and fought his division better than he did," one officer said of Hurlbut. Another wrote to a Freeport newspaper that "the General conducted himself with great gallantry, and his officers and men sustained him heroically." His efforts were not overlooked, as the army promoted him to major general. Hurlbut eventually was given command over the cities of Memphis and New Orleans.

After the war, Hurlbut helped to organize the Grand Army of the Republic and was elected its first national commander. He returned to Belvidere and was elected to the state legislature. He also was a presidential elector for the state in 1868. When Grant became president, he appointed Hurlbut to a diplomatic post as minister to Colombia. While in that South American country, he became interested in the plans to build a canal across Panama to link the Pacific and Atlantic Oceans. Following this mission, he returned to the United States and was twice elected to Congress. He was defeated for a third term. He campaigned for James Garfield in 1880, and following

## Remarkable People and Curious Incidents

Garfield's election to the presidency, Hurlbut was chosen to be the minister to Peru. Although he received a warm welcome in Peru, he didn't serve as minister for long. He died on March 28, 1882.

When Belvidere citizens found out that Hurlbut's body would not return for another month, it gave them time to plan a grand funeral. Those arriving into the city found buildings, homes and edifices draped in black cloth. Each end of the State Street Bridge featured an arch. Trains crammed with passengers began to arrive about noon, bringing the first of about three thousand to come by rail. All of the city's livery stables were filled, and it was estimated that there were twelve thousand mourners. About 1:30 p.m., the procession began in front of the old Adelphia Hall, near the intersection of State and Logan Streets. Three thousand people walked in the funeral procession, which spanned more than a mile and included thirty-six military groups. Hurlbut was laid to rest in Belvidere Cemetery, and his funeral was the largest ever held in Boone County and, possibly, all of northern Illinois.

With such a turnout, it's clear that Hurlbut made an impact locally, nationally and internationally with presidents and statesmen. He also put his trust in men from other strata of society, a characteristic that brings us to the story of Lundy Tuttle. When Hurlbut went to war, he brought three horses with him—Tom, Dick and Harry—as well as Tuttle as his hostler to tend to the horses. Tuttle appears to have been a free black, for he was born in Canada and was part Indian. A photo in a Belvidere newspaper from the

Stephen Hurlbut's horse, one of the three named Tom, Dick and Harry. *Courtesy of the Boone County Historical Museum.*

late 1890s showed a white-bearded Tuttle dressed in boots and bib overalls, wearing an old hat. But what stood out were his massive hands. Perhaps that's what caused Hurlbut to hire Tuttle as his hostler. Descriptions of the general from the Civil War tell that he was "mounted on a beautiful horse" and that he was "well dressed and rode a great horse."

Hurlbut was described at the Battle of Shiloh as riding Dick, a gray stallion, making them both targets for Confederate sharpshooters. One of Hurlbut's horses, perhaps Dick, was shot at Shiloh, and Tuttle said afterward that it was the only time in his life that he cried. "I set up with him all night and took care of him until he got well," he recalled.

Tuttle stayed with Hurlbut through the conflict, even though he never enlisted. At the Siege of Corinth, Tuttle suffered a leg injury when a "grape-shot came whizzin' along and struck the feed box on the wagon." A metal spike spun from the wagon and made Tuttle "pretty lame for a while, let me tell you that."

After the war, Hurlbut, Tuttle and Dick returned to Belvidere. Hurlbut placed his old war horse in the care of George Stevens of Rockford, who looked after the horse until it died on February 6, 1878, at the age of twenty-seven. Dick's death was noted in the *Rockford Journal* and *Belvidere Standard* newspapers. When Hurlbut returned from the war with Dick, he told Stevens to

> *feed, water and faithfully care for the old servant until death should overtake him. That was faithfully done…until old age relieved him of his cares and sent him to those green pastures in the happy land where all good horses go.*

Tuttle outlived both Hurlbut and his favorite horse. Back in Belvidere, Tuttle carved a place in local lore, partly because of his association with a great war hero, but also because he was a hero himself. Tuttle spent so much of his time along the Kishwaukee River that he is credited with saving the lives of thirteen swimmers. It was also Tuttle's duty to fire the cannon on the Fourth of July. He worked at various jobs until he became disabled after falling down a flight of stairs. Tuttle spent the winters at the county poor farm and then would wander into town, saying he would "be right in the spring as soon as the robins get out." Tuttle was found dead one morning in April 1901 outside a saloon, his lunch of two hard-boiled eggs and bread and butter in his hands. A collection was taken up for a proper funeral and burial at Belvidere Cemetery. A story about his funeral said that Tuttle "received honor he never had in his life." Tuttle had two sayings that were remembered. One was the greeting, "Hello, old, boy," and the second was that he wanted to die with his boots on. And that he did.

# Remarkable People and Curious Incidents

It was Boone County's good fortune to have two famous Civil War generals. While Hurlbut made his name on the battlefield and as a politician and statesman, General Allen C. Fuller was influential and widely respected as the adjutant general of all Illinois troops during the Civil War. Fuller was a lawyer and a contemporary of Hurlbut's, arriving in Belvidere in 1846 from Farmington, Connecticut. He practiced law and established himself in local circles as a solid professional and a natural leader who had appropriate social graces. That led to his election, in 1861, as a circuit judge. He soon became recognized as one of the most respected jurists in the state at that time.

With the onset of the war, Governor Yates selected Judge Fuller to become adjutant general for the state and to lead the organization of the military forces needed to fight the Confederacy. At first, the position was thought to be temporary, but as the war progressed and military and civilian leaders realized it was going to be a longer struggle, it was clear that Fuller needed to resign his position on the bench in July 1862. Fuller approached his position as adjutant general with the same energy and vigor that he did his law practice, and as a result, his office ran a smooth operation that was well organized and kept perhaps the best records of any Union state during the war. One of his efforts was to help the families of soldiers fighting in far-off places. When an effort started to contribute funds for these families, Fuller made the first contribution, putting in $500 from his own pocket.

A government survey of the state's military records from the Civil War praised Fuller as follows: "We have thoroughly examined the office of Adjutant General and found it a model in completeness; one that preserves in all its glory the proud record of our soldiery and reflects infinite credit upon [our] Great State." Following his discharge in January 1865, Fuller was elected to the state's General Assembly and eventually served as Speaker of the House. He also was elected to the state senate and twice served as a Republican presidential elector. Fuller became involved in several local businesses, most notably, the National Sewing Machine Company and the Northwestern Shoe Factory. He also helped to found the First and Second National Banks.

Fuller's legacy in Boone County is tangible today, not only because of his deeds and accomplishment but also because of his family. Allen and Nancy Benjamin Fuller had five children, two of whom left lasting legacies. Ida Fuller, Allen and Nancy's youngest child, followed in her father's footsteps in a more feminine way as a performer, according to the *Belvidere Standard* of August 21, 1883. She played the piano at several social and charitable occasions, which were well attended and successful. She graduated from Rockford Seminary (now Rockford College) before she turned twenty. On July 8, 1878, her nineteenth birthday, Ida Fuller married T. Adelbert (Dell) Hovey in a high social event that included a Chicago caterer and dancing at the Fuller home on Van Buren Street until nearly midnight.

Ida Hovey continued to play the piano at charitable events and traveled in significant social circles. She and her husband often hosted social events at their home. On December 26, 1881, more than two hundred people attended a masquerade ball at the courthouse. Described as "one of the most brilliant and thoroughly enjoyable affairs ever given in this city," the guests kept their masks intact until the grand march finished about 11:30 p.m. The dancing continued until 4:00 a.m., and Ida Hovey's costume was the hit of the evening. She wore red satin trimmed with gold sequins and carried a tambourine. Dell was dressed as a "Highland laddie."

One of the most spirited and effervescent individuals in Boone County history had a short life, unfortunately. In August 1888, word reached Boone County from Bayfield, Wisconsin, that Ida Fuller Hovey had died at the age of twenty-four. The cause was the same illness that took her older brother Wilbur's life: consumption, known today as tuberculosis. In her obituary, the *Belvidere Standard* reported that the disease spread rapidly:

> *Only a few short months ago the bloom of health was on her cheek and her eyes sparked with joyous life. Her life has been fair sailing overspread with sunny skies. The idol of a kind, indulgent father and surrounded by circles of friends, she was one who won and turned tenderest regards.*

Late in 1883, General Allen Fuller, who idolized his daughter, donated $5,000 to the City of Belvidere to start the community's first public library. It was a memorial to his daughter, Ida Fuller Hovey, with the request that the library be named in her honor. The first Ida Public Library was in a room on the second floor of the former Belvidere City Hall, now the home of the State Street Fire Station. After twenty years, the library received a gift from the Andrew Carnegie Foundation, and in 1913, Ida Public Library opened at the corner of North State and Madison Streets.

The other Fuller legacy is not as well known, but it is significant in its contribution, nonetheless. Fuller's last remaining child, Katherine or Kitty, married Thomas Rhinehart. They had two children—Ida, named after

# Remarkable People and Curious Incidents

Kitty's sister, and Frank. Frank stepped into the family business, starting as an assistant cashier at the First National Bank, which his grandfather founded, and was working his way up when the United States went to war in 1917. Frank resigned from the bank on December 7, 1917, and enlisted in the army. He was stationed at Camp Grant in Rockford, where he worked in the motor pool and eventually was promoted to sergeant. He was at Camp Grant when the great influenza epidemic struck, killing more than fourteen hundred soldiers. As the truck sergeant, he had the task of transporting the bodies for burial. He was diligent in his duties, and despite being exposed to the virus, he never contracted the disease. Frank Rhinehart was discharged in 1919 and became involved in the organization and building of the Apollo Theatre in downtown Belvidere.

It is a small story in comparison to his grandfather's, and coupled with Ida's, it sheds some light on the impact Allen Fuller made on Boone County. He died at his home on Van Buren Street on December 6, 1901.

# Crimes, Crime Fighters and Strange Legends

They say you can hear strange things at night out in southwestern Boone County, where Bloods Point Road meets Irene Road. It's a local teenage tradition to trek out there and walk the spooky landscape of Bloods Point Cemetery, especially at Halloween. There are stories of bloodcurdling screams, bloody school buses and Arthur Blood's ghost roaming the land he used to call home. But they are nothing more than stories.

There was an Arthur Blood, said to be the first permanent white settler in Flora Township. After he claimed his land, he went to Dixon's Ferry to register it, paying $1.25 for each quarter section of land. In an area that was protected by a line of timber, he built two log cabins. Then he left and was lost forever to history. However, his name lived on, in the cemetery, a creamery and a road, Bloods Point. Anything beyond that is legend.

Another enduring local legend is that of the day that the famous outlaw Jesse James and his gang swooped into Spring Township, Boone County. Many people swore that there was truth to this story and believe it still; many years ago, a group placed a wooden sign south of Interstate 90 on Fern Hill Road that read: "Jesse James camped here." The story that appeared in local histories related that in 1876, James and his gang camped on the banks of Mosquito Creek in eastern Boone County. While camping, they purchased supplies at the nearby home of the Sullivans, and they paid in gold coins. The gang left the next day on its way to Minnesota, where several members were caught in a botched bank holdup.

There are different versions of the tale. One says that the outlaws camped on the Kishwaukee River near the former village of Newburg. Another claimed that the gang members gave members of the Sullivan family a white horse in exchange for food. None of the stories answer questions like why wanted men would camp out in the open where they could be seen or, if they had gold coins to hand out, why they camped near a mosquito-infested creek when there were hotel beds in nearby Belvidere. And how common was it for a group of men to be camping in the open, long after the land had been claimed?

Before he died, John Powell lived on land uphill from the place on Mosquito Creek where the outlaws were said to have camped. Long before his home was built, a Sullivan family did live up the road a bit, and Powell said that one of the Sullivan boys, Henry, told him the following story:

> *Henry lived in a house over there when he was young. One day, his mother gave him some fresh baked bread to bring down to some men who were camped out on Mosquito Creek. They gave him some gold coins and told him they were from the Jesse James Gang. They were on their way to Minnesota, where they got all shot up.*

Powell said he heard the story in 1942, and there are some clues that at least part of it is authentic.

The 1880 census lists Henry as one of six children of Timothy and Rose Sullivan. When Tim died in 1910, his obituary said that he "lived for a while in the town of Spring, where he bought a farm." That would put the family in a home near where the incident supposedly took place. But was Henry telling him what he saw or what one of his brothers saw? Henry was two years old at the time of the 1880 census, so he wasn't yet born in 1876. But he did have two older brothers: John, born in 1872, and Timothy, born in 1875.

The James-Coulter Gang is credited with twenty-five robberies and holdups of banks, railroads and stagecoaches. The gang's range of misdeeds was cast from Minnesota to Texas to West Virginia. The gangsters robbed a bank in Adair, Iowa, in 1873, and botched a bank robbery in Northfield, Minnesota, on September 7, 1876, when Jim, Cole and Bob Younger were captured and three other men were killed.

Until Bob Ford killed him on April 3, 1882, Jesse James was credited not only with more crimes but also good deeds. One of the stories appears to be taken from Robin Hood's catalogue. It starts with a poor widow unable to make her mortgage payment. When a stranger comes by, she invites him to lunch. When he leaves, he pays with a fifty-dollar gold coin, and the widow uses the money to pay the landlord. When the landlord leaves the widow's home, the stranger robs him of his fifty dollars—and the robber is Jesse James.

A few other facts need to be noted. The James-Coulter Gang did wander far and wide, and it is possible that it passed through northern Illinois. This was a time when it was common for homeless men to stop at farmhouses and ask for a meal in exchange for work. The most likely scenario went this way: A group of men camped out on Mosquito Creek in 1876 and asked for food from a nearby farmhouse. When the two youngest Sullivan boys brought the meat and bread to the men, they may have seen them shooting targets or talking boastfully. One of the boys may have asked, "Are you from the James Gang." And one on of the men probably winked at the boy and said, "Yes, we are, son. But promise you won't tell a soul." The boy shook his head and said, "No, I won't ever, ever tell."

The final word on this legend was found in a clipping from the *Belvidere Standard* dated Tuesday, April 11, 1882. Next to a story about the death of Civil War general Stephen A. Hurlbut is a small piece that reads, "Jesse James, the noted train robber and outlaw, of Missouri, was shot in his own house by one Ford, also a member of the band of train robbers." Nowhere in the story does it mention or hint that James may have camped out one night in Boone County.

While the Jesse James story may be pure legend, another is 100 percent factual, and when it occurred, it was one of the most famous crimes of the era in the state. And it occurred in one of Boone County's smallest communities, Garden Prairie.

In 1881, Garden Prairie had a train station on the Chicago and North Western Railroad. The depot agent was Daniel Stott, who had many health problems, but he also had a pretty, young wife, Julia. Reports vary as to Stott's illness (it could have been epilepsy), but his wife dutifully traveled to Chicago by train for his medicine. It was after one of these trips that Daniel Stott died suddenly. There must have been talk in the community—for example, why would Julia travel to Chicago for medicine when Belvidere, and even Rockford, were closer? Something caused Boone County coroner Dr. Frank S. Whitman to suspect foul play, so he obtained the medicine that Mrs. Stott obtained in Chicago. When Whitman gave some of the medicine to a dog, the results were astonishing. The dog died. Stott had been poisoned.

Further investigation revealed that Mrs. Stott had been seen boarding the train to Chicago the night before Stott's death, and she had been spotted in the Garden Prairie depot with a mysterious man shortly after her husband was buried. Mrs. Stott was brought in for questioning by Boone

Simon's drawing of Daniel Stott's gravestone in Garden Prairie Cemetery. *Courtesy Gary Simon.*

Gravestone of Daniel Stott in the Garden Prairie Cemetery. *Photo by author.*

# Remarkable People and Curious Incidents

County state's attorney R.W. Coone, and when questioned, she admitted she was having a love affair with Dr. Thomas N. Cream of Chicago. Then she clammed up. Dr. Cream was brought to Belvidere for questioning, and sensing he was in trouble, he bolted out a window to try to escape. He fell through the window, but right into the arms of a policeman. After Stott's body was exhumed and found to contain strychnine, Mrs. Stott cut a deal. She agreed to testify against Dr. Cream in exchange for charges against her being dropped. Dr. Cream was convicted in a trial that lasted one day and sentenced to life imprisonment. However, he was paroled after ten years and moved to Canada.

That, however, wasn't the end of Dr. Cream's crimes, which could have become legendary if not for another notorious killer. After moving to Canada, Dr. Cream went to England, where he was convicted of poisoning three young girls. Again, he used strychnine. This time, there was no escape or parole—he was hanged. One local legend claims that someone heard Dr. Cream's last words. As the trapdoor opened to plummet him to death, he reportedly said, "I'm Jack…" Was he identifying himself as Jack the Ripper? But Jack the Ripper's killing spree was from August 31 to November 9, 1888. Dr. Cream was serving a prison sentence in the United States at that time.

Arthur Blood is not the only source of local ghost stories. There's also the legend of Nellie Dunton. As the legend has been told, Dunton was jilted by her fiancé just before their wedding and, in a fit of despair, donned her white wedding dress, waded into the Kishwaukee River and drowned. Her home on Lincoln Avenue east of State Street along the river is said to be haunted with unusual and unexplained noises and locked doors that suddenly swing open. This much is true: Dunton drowned in the Kishwaukee River in 1920. But there is a more logical explanation.

Dunton lived with her respectable family on Lincoln Avenue and was considered well mannered and well read. However, in her later years, she suffered from insomnia, was a sleepwalker and had trouble seeing. On the night of June 29, 1920, the Duntons' maid heard a strange sound about midnight. Thinking it was Nellie sleepwalking, the maid dismissed the noise and went back to sleep. The next day when Nellie failed to come to breakfast, the maid called for help. With the help of a neighbor, she searched the house and found no sign of the woman. The neighbor then noticed footsteps on the wet ground leading to the river. They followed them and found Nellie facedown in the river. A coroner's inquest found that she had died of a tragic accident. She probably was sleepwalking. Disoriented and unable to see, she probably stumbled into the river and was unable to free herself from the muddy bottom. Those who said she took her own life were refuted by her brother, George Dunton. He said that Nellie was deathly afraid of snakes, and a newspaper account of the time reported that small snakes were commonly found along the riverbanks.

---

If Simon P. Doty wasn't the busiest man in the early days of Boone County, he was certainly one of them. Among his firsts was that he was the first sheriff, but other law enforcement officers had original stories to tell.

The first of those stories belongs to Ormond Hayden, who was elected to become the first constable when LeRoy Township had its first elections in 1837. Hayden's claim to the post was that he owned the only horse in the township. But it turned out the beast wasn't a horse; it was a brindled ox. People thought it was a horse because it was saddle-broken and was a fast trotter, able to make "3:20 in the slough."

Sarah T. Ames provided another original crime-fighting story. For years, she was known for her women's hat shop in downtown Belvidere. Before she became a milliner, she was one of the toughest law enforcement officers in county history. Sarah's husband, Albert T. Ames, served as Boone County sheriff for ten years. As soon as Albert took office, he swore in his wife as a chief deputy sheriff because he wanted someone close to him whom he could trust. It was a good choice.

By her own account, she spent many nights in the jailhouse, with twenty to thirty men in cells, accompanied only by a servant. But she had a keen eye and ear. Once she noticed that the men in the lockup were doing an extraordinary amount of dancing. A newspaper account of the day read that she noticed two men were "continually on the floor, and I noticed that they kept their jigs [even] while the sweat was rolling off them." Suspecting that something was up, she positioned herself out of sight and listened carefully. While the men were loudly dancing up a storm, she heard another distinct sound. "It was caused by the drawing of a file across a hard surface." Immediately, she knew that the men were digging some kind of hole and had hatched an escape plot.

"Calling my husband, we entered one of the cells from which the noise proceeded," she said. "Under the bed, we found an excavation large enough to pass the whole gang." The hole was covered well enough so that the work went undetected. While two men danced to create a diversion with loud sounds, others scraped away at the hole in the floor, stashing the stone and dirt into the cloth encasings of the mattresses and pillows.

Albert served well for eight years, but during his last two years of office, he became ill, and Sarah took over the duties as sheriff. Even though she still held the post of chief deputy, there was no doubt that she was in charge, as she arrested several criminals at the point of a gun.

Once, she tracked an escaped criminal nearly one thousand miles. "A fifteen-year-old boy once led me on the longest chase I ever had," she said. "He was sort of a trustee and one day, he disappeared. I got track of him and followed him nine hundred miles over the states of Iowa and Illinois. I overtook him in the southern part of Illinois and brought him back to Belvidere."

Another time, she chased two men who also had escaped from jail. She rode after them on horseback, carrying a shotgun, and caught up with them southeast of Belvidere near Fern Hill Road. The two men walked back to Belvidere ahead of Sarah, who held them at gunpoint while she rode her horse.

And there was the time she thwarted a gang of unruly men who were threatening to take over a hallway in the courthouse.

"Quit this right away!" Sarah bellowed to them. "All of you will have to go to your cells and be locked up until you learn how to behave."

"I'd like to see you stop us," said the group's ringleader, described as a "heavy-set criminal with an ugly disposition."

"Maybe I can't," said Sarah. "But this can," she continued, whipping out a pistol and leveling it at the prisoners.

The men turned and walked wordlessly back to their cells.

# Hairbreadth Harry, the King of the Hobos

If not for pictures, one would swear that the story of Hairbreadth Harry was pure Boone County fiction. A poetry-reading wanderer who rode the rails, boasted of taking seven baths a day and often walked backward is the stuff of legends, but it is all true. And he truly is a Boone County original.

His real name was James Joseph Moan, and he was born on a farm in southern Boone County in June 1881. When he was seventeen, he left his family. At first, he worked around town and did odd jobs. When he was twenty-five, he began a life of roaming, mostly in Iowa. His return to Belvidere was often written up in the local newspapers, and he put many of his life experiences on paper with a book of poems he wrote in 1934. He was twice crowned "King of the Hobos" in Britt, Iowa, and died of pneumonia on April 14, 1947, in Bennett, Iowa.

In his book, *The Life, History, and Poetry of Hairbreadth Harry* (or *Old Inner Tubes Comes Clean*), he wrote that he was the family's "black sheep" but that his heart was light, not dark. He was proud of his family. "Back in Belvidere where I was born and raised, they will tell you my folks were the finest in the land," he wrote. However, he admitted that he was spoiled as a child:

> *I was spoiled in my youth, as I was the pride and joy of the household and friends. I had my own way. My demands were always granted, and they were many and insistent. I had to have my own knife and Auntie's spoon or I wouldn't eat at all. Many's the time my mother got up at midnight and milked the cow to get me some fresh milk. The fact is, I was hard to suit. If I had got more of the whip and less coddling, there wouldn't have been any Hairbreadth Harry.*

Riding the rails was once acceptable in America, and soon Harry began his rail wandering. If he was spoiled as a youth, he was peculiar as an adult. He said he got his name for his penchant for cleanliness: "I started writing articles…saying I took seven baths a day…and was called the cleanest man in the state." That habit led to his name because he was said to be clean down to a breadth of a hair. One of his idiosyncrasies was a habit of walking backward. He said he did it because his right leg had been poisoned by shoe dye. In fact, he said both legs were poisoned in this way. "I was poisoned with shoe dye in the right leg. Before it was cured, my left leg was poisoned and still is. [That is] the reason for my sandals and fame."

His footwear did indeed become infamous. He wore burlap bags or old inner tubes tied to his feet by burlap strips or twine. Contemporary photos of Harry show this distinctive footwear. Other times, he walked barefoot. On that subject he wrote:

> *They say Hairbreadth Harry walks backward*
> *That he does it to favor his leg.*
> *That if he didn't walk backwards*
> *He'd soon be wearing a peg.*
> *Hairbreadth Harry, the man who walks backwards,*
> *Who can't take his eyes off a scene*
> *When he meets a pretty girl, he walks backwards.*
> *And, sometimes, the police treat him mean.*
> *Sometimes he tells them he wants to see where he came from,*
> *Or that he is low on gasoline.*

One of the stories told about him was that he often bathed in gasoline. With a woolen cap on his head, a white beard, a great coat around him and a cane to help him walk, he certainly was quite a sight, and his frequent appearances in town made news. A March 28, 1935 story in a Belvidere newspaper reports:

> *Hairbreadth Harry is returning to the old home town. From the west today… Freeport to be exact…comes the word that his pilgrimage homeward has extended that far and most any day now the barefoot one will undoubtedly be seen on the streets here again.*

When Harry returned to Belvidere, he often stayed on Hobo Island, a small piece of land where Piscasaw Creek meets the Kishwaukee River

## Remarkable People and Curious Incidents

near the railroad tracks east of town. It was a traditional gathering place for hobos, vagrants and other "Knights of the Road" until it was destroyed by an enterprising sheriff.

Hairbreadth's Harry's visits to Belvidere made news because they were news. On one trip, he wandered into the Scriven School in Spring Township and startled the students and their teacher, Miss Vowles. Harry had attended that one-room school as a child, and the teacher later wrote:

> *He asked if he might be allowed to come in and look around. Hairbreadth Harry was a Moan who lived down the road. He had a shock of red bushy hair and a full beard of red. His clothes were ragged and he had gunny sacks tied with twine for shoes. I was a little skeptical about letting him in, but told him he could. He came in and told us about where he had traveled. The children asked him questions and we all enjoyed it. Later he wrote a book of poems and sent us one. He had a stanza about his visit to the school.*

It read:

> *I came to the old schoolhouse*
> *Miss Vowles let me in*
> *With gunny sacks on my feet*
> *And whiskers on my chin*
> *The children asked me quite a bit*
> *Hairbreadth Harry was a hit.*

His appearances weren't always so welcomed. The 1935 newspaper story relates how Harry had not been seen since the previous summer, "when he and the police had a disagreement concerning the garb in which he appeared." Or, better yet, it probably was what he wasn't wearing. "At that time, Harry was told what he must do sartorially if he wanted to remain… or else…and so it was the 'or else.' It was said that he went west to start a nudist colony."

An article in the *Belvidere Daily Republican* in 1963 retold the story of his return trips to Boone County:

> *Hairbreadth is remembered by many older residents of the city and addressed various civic clubs to relate his experiences as a hobo. "Hobo Island" attracted many "Knights of the Road" during the tough days of the depression. For the most part, they were well treated by residents of this area.*

A color poster of Hairbreadth Harry at the Boone County Historical Museum. *Photo by author.*

In one of his poems, Harry told of a hobo gathering in Boone County, which he called the "1936 Belvidere Blowout." The nicknames of his fellow travelers are a lost part of Americana. In part, the poem read:

*Come all you rambling rounders,*
*And listen while I hum,*
*About a party held at Belvidere*
*By the "Great American Bum."*

# Remarkable People and Curious Incidents

*Some came in by highway*
*And some came by passenger train,*
*And the rest came by box car,*
*But all were treated just the same.*
*So here's to "Bacon Butt Shorty,"*
*Our hats are off to you.*
*You threw a darn nice party,*
*And drove away all the blues.*
*There were "Molder Joe" and "Seven Below,"*
*And the well-known "Salem Slim."*
*"Tin Can Red" and "Sick Abed,"*
*And old time "Madison Jim."*
*"Hot Shot Al" and "Old Pal, Old Pal,"*
*And an old time stiff called "Scotty."*
*"D.C. Joe" and a "Mile to Go,"*
*And a bo called "Hotsy Totsy."*
*From "Circuit 66" came "Billy Hicks,"*
*Along with the "Janesville Kid,"*
*"Wiggins Patch" and "Johnny Hatch,"*
*And they all pried off the lid.*
*"Old Bill Doaks" and other soaks,*
*Came down these "Golden Stairs,"*
*Some came in bunches,*
*And some came down in pairs.*
*The hometown boys came down in force,*
*They thought Santa Claus had hit town.*
*But there were mighty few*
*Who could out drink the crew*
*For they had not been around.*
*For those box car tramps*
*Had drank in camps,*
*And some in foreign ports.*
*They could throw their feet*
*When they had to eat,*
*They were 100 percent sports.*
*The alcohol came in gallon lots,*
*And barrels full of beer.*
*The tobacco came in arm loads,*
*To cause the boys much cheer.*

The only known photo of Hairbreadth Harry. *Courtesy of the Boone County Historical Museum.*

Harry was crowned "King of the Hobos" at national hobo conventions in Britt, Iowa, and he used that fame to seek national office. In 1936, he called for a state convention for his "Third Horse" Party in Des Moines. He declared himself a presidential candidate on the platform of "working the other horse."

If Harry had lived in the early twenty-first century, he undoubtedly would be communicating with the latest electronic paths. He certainly would have had his own blog because most of his writing was about himself. He wrote:

> *Hello, Hairbreadth Harry? Who are you?*
> *Are you human, cannibal, or divine?*
> *Are you an imp from Hell,*
> *A fallen angel or a lost soul?*
> *Is your mission in life to destroy the farm*
> *Or destroy the poison in your leg?*
> *Do you walk backwards or forwards?*
> *How often do you eat?*
> *Is it true that the girls all fall for you?*

# Remarkable People and Curious Incidents

*Do you like blonds or brunettes?*
*What are your faults and frailties?*

When Harry's book was released in 1934, the *Belvidere Daily Republican* wrote a short, tongue-in-cheek article. Its poetry, it read, was "written in his inimitable style…yes, there are reams and reams of it and not a little about Hairbreadth, himself, personally." Harry obviously loved Boone County and Belvidere, and when he wasn't writing about himself, he wrote about his favorite residents, whose names are distant memories. There was Harold Sewell:

*They'll lead Sewell up on the mountain*
*And show him the fields of gold.*
*They'll tell him it's for the taking,*
*If he'll follow in their fold.*
*But they'll be wasting their time on Harold,*
*For Harold G. Sewell's sold.*
*He's Hairbreadth Harry's Lawyer,*
*And they couldn't buy him with gold."*

Of Hugh R. Dysart, he wrote: "We like his smiling face / who cheers us with his presence / His pleasing style and grace." And "three cheers" for Mabel E. Crull, "who typed for Hairbreadth, the poet / whose head ached and her arm weary / as far in the night she wrote." Mayor Mark I. Butler "treated Hairbreadth royally."

Harry's roaming days ended at the age of sixty-six. He died at the fire station in Bennett, Iowa, and is buried there. The county paid for his funeral expenses.

# The Eldredge

## *The Little Car that Couldn't*

Workers at the National Sewing Machine Company wondered why the 6:45 a.m. whistle didn't blow on the morning of November 29, 1911. When they arrived at work at the sprawling plant that manufactured sewing machines, bicycles, washing machines and other products, they found the doors locked and the main entrance draped in mourning. Word quickly spread that Barnabas Eldredge, founder and president of the National Sewing Machine Company, had died the day before in Chicago, thus ending the significant impact this local industrial giant had on Belvidere and Boone County. While the man was gone, the company he founded stayed in business for four decades, and its legacy continues today.

Barnabas Eldredge was born on June 18, 1843, with a mechanical and pragmatic mind, which led him into manufacturing after the Civil War. About 1865, he started a hardware store in Cleveland, Ohio. He had a brother who worked for the Domestic Sewing Machine Company in Detroit, so in 1869, he sold his hardware store and moved to Michigan. Eldredge became a general manager in Chicago, where he got a feel for the needs of his territory, which ranged from Ohio to the Rocky Mountains and the South. With that experience, he struck out on his own.

He took his ideas to the Northeast, where most sewing machine makers and other major manufactures were traditionally located. Seeking a place to build his new model, he got his start at the Ames Manufacturing Company in Chicopee Falls, Massachusetts. From the start, he was never willing to settle for small achievements. Because of his experience with his brother's company, he was aware of the new markets opening up in the

One of only a few models of the Eldredge automobile built in Belvidere by the National Sewing Machine Company. It can be seen at the Boone County Historical Museum. *Photo by author.*

West, so he moved to Chicago, where he became partners with the June Manufacturing Company.

F.T. June's company used expired patents from industry-leader Singer Sewing Machine Company to manufacture inexpensive knockoffs of Singers called the Jennie June. Eldredge had developed a competitive sewing machine, which was seen as a strong model by his competitors, so he was unable to obtain funding for its manufacture. In Chicago, June's model was not selling well, so he entered into an agreement with Eldredge to make the latter's new machine. For a few years, the company produced Jennie Junes and Eldredge's Barnabas-E Model, with Barnabas Eldredge as vice-president. In a short time, the June Manufacturing Company was making far more of Eldredge's model, the Barnabas-E, than Jenny Junes.

Sensing an opportunity, Eldredge made a move. One story said that he left Chicago to avoid labor strife; another said that he was seeking skilled workers, who could be found in the Boone County community. There is documentation that labor strife was prevalent in Chicago, including

# Remarkable People and Curious Incidents

Scheidenhelm's drawing of the Eldredge. *Courtesy Kit Scheidenhelm.*

A late nineteenth-century photo of the National Sewing Machine Company. *Courtesy of the Boone County Historical Museum.*

anarchist riots and strikes. For whatever reason, Eldredge and June moved the entire operation to a two-story building in Belvidere in 1886. When F.T. June died in 1890, Eldredge consolidated the two businesses into the National Sewing Machine Company.

The National didn't stay in that two-story building for long. The company grew so large along the southern bank of the Kishwaukee River that, at its peak, it covered more than two hundred acres. In 1900, it built a foundry along the banks of the Kishwaukee, and in 1928, it built a steam-driven generator building. And it was always forward thinking. In 1894, it purchased the Freeport Bicycle Manufacturing Company and moved its entire operation to Belvidere at a time when bicycles were popular with the public. Its two-wheeler, the Eldredge, won a six-hour bicycle race at Madison Square Garden. When automobiles were the latest rage, the National built two models. It also built Happy Day washing machines, vices, food grinders and toys.

The National was one of the first manufacturers to make specialty brands for individual customers. It sold its sewing machines with the brand names of Macy's, Marshall Field's and Montgomery Ward, among others. Not only did it make a variety of products, but it also made all of the parts of the product. As Eldredge said more than once, "We make these machines from the pig-iron up." At the time, it was said that the National was the only factory in the world that made all of the attachments of its products in the

A postcard view of the National Sewing Machine Company. *Courtesy of the Boone County Historical Museum.*

## Remarkable People and Curious Incidents

company's buildings on South State Street. And it was a good place to work. It is said that jobs were offered for life. In 1939, a report indicated that more than one hundred people were working past their retirement age. Instead of shutting down during the Depression, the National switched to making cast-iron toys, the Vindex Line.

Harold Neff, who ran the Vindex Line, explained the reasoning in a letter dated March 5, 1970, to the Still Bank Collectors Club of America. Neff wrote:

> *Early in the 1930s the depression hit our industry like it did all others in the U.S.A. and our sales of Sewing and Washing machines were badly depressed. We wanted to be able to retain as many of our employees as was possible and began to try and produce other lines of goods that would give work to our people.*

Neff, who worked for National from 1916 to 1951, wrote that the National made a complete line of home workshop items, including lathes, band saws, jigsaws, saw tables and line shaft assemblies. It also decided to make cast-iron toys and novelties.

> *The line was quite complete, we had negotiated with Oldsmobile and Pontiac to copy their line of cars in miniature as well as Harley Davidson motor cycles and side cars. Also we made a Power Shovel in*

Twentieth-century aerial photo of the National Sewing Machine Company. *Courtesy of the Boone County Historical Museum.*

*miniature...and a complete line of Farm Machinery as made by John Deere Co. All of these companies used our toy numbers with their dealers for display purposes but gave us permission to market the lines to whom we cared to sell.*

Other Vindex items included bookends, table lamps, dog doorstops and owl and dog banks.

Vindex toys were made from the early 1930s to the early 1940s, when the company switched to producing material for World War II. Today, Vindex toys are collectibles, with some items, such as the John Deer threshing machine, selling for $4,500.

The National continued to adapt in the twentieth century. It claimed to make the first electric sewing machine in 1917 and, in 1935, introduced a model that sewed in both directions. An aluminum model followed in 1939. But its reign as a midwestern industrial giant ended after World War II. With too much competition from other markets, including Japan, the National shut its doors for good in 1953.

When the Chrysler Assembly Plant was built in the mid-1960s in Belvidere and began operation in 1965, many people believed it was the first auto manufacturer in the county. But they forgot about the Runabout. Barnabas Eldredge was always eager to cash in on the latest consumer desire. He made bicycles at the peak of interest, and his strategy almost worked again with

Artists conception of the Chrysler Assembly Plant that was built in Belvidere in the mid-1960s. *Courtesy of the Boone County Historical Museum.*

# Remarkable People and Curious Incidents

Chrysler chairman Lee Iacocca speaks with workers at the plant, 1989. *Courtesy of the Boone County Historical Museum.*

the automobile. At the turn of the twentieth century, he put his engineers to work designing an inexpensive light auto.

In 1901, the National built a new addition to its grounds off South State Street. The opening of the new addition was heralded with a huge ball, the largest social event at the time in Belvidere. In 1904, Eldredge unveiled the E Runabout, which had a horizontally mounted, air-cooled, single-cylinder engine that generated about eight horsepower. With the engine under the seat, it had a three-speed transmission and seated two. The cost was $750, and it was an attractive machine. Its slogan was "Just What It Ought to Be." But with eight horsepower, it just did not have enough oomph. Models were unable to climb the little hill on Whitney Boulevard behind the U.S. Post Office. Eldredge made another model, the 1904 Tonneau or Eldredge Touring Car, which had a rear seat that could be reached only from the rear.

This auto boosted output with a four-cylinder engine and sixteen horsepower and sold for $2,000. Eldredges were among the first vehicles made with a left-handed steering wheel. They were made until 1906, when National yielded success to Detroit. The 1906 model featured ten horsepower and double rear wheel brakes and sold for $750. But the last of the line was sold for $450, and a newspaper advertisement included the following

Aerial view of the Chrysler Assembly Plant. *Courtesy of the Boone County Historical Museum.*

Chrysler chairman Lee Iacocca visits Chrysler Assembly Plant in 1989. *Courtesy of the Boone County Historical Museum.*

ad: "Never Again Will You Have an Opportunity like this to purchase a machine that is thoroughly well made, and in every way First-Class." Who knew that Belvidere would once again become a place where automobiles were assembled?

# Remarkable People and Curious Incidents

This occurred in 1965, when the Chrysler Assembly Plant began producing cars and became the county's largest employer. Boone County has always been involved in production. Over the years, it has manufactured scales, wire products, beauty salon equipment and ice cream, among other products. Its farmland is considered to be some of the best in the country and produces abundant crops of corn and soybeans. The farms and factories were the draw for the three main immigrant groups that came into Boone County.

# "Hundreds of Heroes"

A local Indian legend holds that what is now Boone County was created as a sacred place, a sanctuary, a hunting ground and a place to grow food, and no natural disaster would befall it—unless a small ridge on the west side of the Kishwaukee River near the Winnebago County line was disturbed. One definition of the Indian word *Kishwaukee* is "free from storms."

Geography has had a lot to do with Boone County's aversion to natural disasters, such as tornados. Although the landscape features mostly prairies, there are hills to the southeast and northwest, creating a southwest-northeast notch. Unless a major storm hits directly in that notch, most storms generally slide north or south of the major population areas. Shaw Road runs north–south less than a mile from the eastern Winnebago County line. It used to run straight to a "T" with Newburg Road. However, in the mid-twentieth century, Shaw was rerouted slightly several yards to the west, where it now meets Newburg Road. Construction of the new road meant that the small ridge that the Indians held sacred was disturbed.

While that may be a legend, there is no doubt about what occurred in Belvidere on a hot, humid Friday afternoon one spring. On April 21, 1967, a killer tornado swept through the central part of the county and into south and southeastern Belvidere. It may have formed within sight of the sacred Indian ground, but once it did, it raked across nearly the width of the county, starting west of Irene Road and finally lifting into the clouds for good near Garden Prairie Road, ten miles away. It caught the southwest-northeast crease cleanly. When it was over, twenty-four people were dead, including seventeen children; more than five hundred more were injured; and more

Yunk's drawing of the aftermath of the 1967 tornado. The letters on Belvidere High School were damaged in this way. *Courtesy Troy Yunk.*

than one hundred homes and twelve businesses were destroyed, with hundreds more damaged. The loss was estimated at $25 million (close to $50 million today). It remains the single worst storm to hit northern Illinois, and its memory is never far from residents' thoughts even today.

The storm smacked into Belvidere and struck or damaged the Chrysler Assembly Plant, the Pacemaker Food Store, Highland Hospital, Belvidere High School, Immanuel Lutheran School and DeWane's Livestock Exchange. In a span of three minutes, from about 3:49 to 3:52 p.m., the tornado bore down on the high school, where elementary, junior and senior high school students were leaving for the day or getting onto buses, and then took off for Immanuel Lutheran, where students were also leaving for the weekend. From there, it went to DeWane's, which was having its weekly animal auction. From DeWane's, the tornado continued on its northeasterly path, slicing through fields on its way out of Boone

# Remarkable People and Curious Incidents

The monument to the Belvidere Tornado of April 21, 1967, at Belvidere High School. *Photo by author.*

County. The person who may have been the last to be injured as the tornado moved out of Boone County had one of the most remarkable survivor stories to surface from the disaster.

Gary Turner was a thirty-four-year-old farmer and father of three who farmed on Lawrenceville Road with his wife, Anne. Today, when we hear about storm chasers and see the stunning videos these daring people record, we must remember the story of Gary Turner, who tried to do the opposite. Instead of chasing the Belvidere Tornado, he drove his pickup truck in reverse up Lawrenceville Road. Needless to say, nature won.

Turner was a dairy farmer. On that April day, he was west of his buildings, repairing a fence. "I was going to use it for my young heifers to keep them on pasture and grass near the buildings and near water," he said.

It was so warm that day that he took off his jacket, and as he worked, he noticed clouds building up to the far west. "But, they just looked like, you know, storms that come here annually in northern Illinois. It really didn't concern me too much." Turner was nailing the barbed-wire fence to a post when he realized he had run out of staples. He checked the time, not quite 4:00 p.m., too soon to milk the cows (that was about 5:30 p.m.), but just enough time to run to the Farm and Fleet store in Belvidere to buy more staples. He left the fence and walked to his pickup truck, a blue 1961 Chevrolet half-ton that he bought at a farm sale. Then he took off for town, turning west onto Lawrenceville. He had just passed his ridge of evergreens to the south when he noticed something odd.

"All of a sudden, I looked out into the field about a half mile away, and there was a big cloud of dirt on the ground," he said. "I never actually saw a funnel cloud. It was to the southwest of us, and it was rolling on the ground, and I was startled by it."

In a split second, Turner made a decision to stay in the truck. It was, he said,

> *a life-changing event. I never thought about getting out of my truck. I think I should have jumped out of my truck and ran somewhere, not so much into a building, but found a hole somewhere that I could have jumped into, or a basement. I was concerned about being in harm's way, and I wasn't thinking. I thought the storm would be kind of narrow, so I put the truck in reverse and started backing up east, not turning the truck around. I didn't think I had time to do that.*

As the storm began to catch up with him, Turner kept rolling his Chevy pickup backward down Lawrenceville Road, past his house and farm and past the Flueger Farm, which was a quarter mile east of his farm. He had just reached the Henninger Farm when he "saw all of the shingles and things starting to fly from that yard, things just taking off. That's the last thing I knew."

When the tornado caught up to him, Turner quickly tried to drop to the floor. "I thought, 'Oh, boy, I'd better hit the floor of the truck.'" But it was too late. "I went to throw myself down because I thought the doors would come open." As he was trying to get down, the truck flipped over, and he went through the window on the passenger side, headfirst. "My head hit the window, but my teeth hit the window sill of the truck." The impact knocked him out as the truck was blown into a ten-inch utility pole. He can't remember how long he was unconscious, perhaps as many as fifteen minutes. "I got out of the truck and looked around, and it was just as quiet as it could be, just no wind. I looked to the north and didn't see any sign of the storm."

At first, he had no idea where he was; then he noticed the Flueger Farm—or what was left of it. "The barn was gone, and they had quite a few buildings there, but they were gone." He started walking, not stopping at his own house because he knew no one was home.

> *I walked back down the road and got to my uncle's house, which is directly across the street from mine. I walked up the driveway, and saw my uncle's house was cockeyed, and his buildings were gone. And there sat his car, right by the house…it didn't even move, but the barn and the buildings were all blown away.*

Turner did notice that the back window of his uncle's car was blown out. Then he saw his uncle come out of the basement. "He took one look at me and said, 'Well, we'd better get you to the hospital.'" Until that moment, Turner didn't realize he had been injured. "I really didn't feel any pain," he said. "I guess I didn't have any pain. We got in the car and took off."

Turner's uncle asked, "Where are we going?"

Turner answered, "We'll go to Highland Hospital. Anne will look for me at Highland Hospital."

The two men drove into Belvidere and got to the downtown Y intersection, where State Street and Logan Avenue meet. They turned south onto South State in the direction of Highland Hospital and that's when they saw a nurse. "She was stumbling up the street," Turner said.

> *Her uniform was all dirty, and she had this blank stare on her face, and I said, "That don't look good. We'd better go to St. Joe's." So we turned around and went to St. Joe's. About then, I realized that my top teeth were gone. They just broke off. Just broke right off.*

St. Joseph's Hospital was in the northeastern part of Belvidere, an area generally unaffected by the tornado. When Turner and his uncle arrived, the emergency room was quiet. "I was basically the first patient that went into the emergency room," he said. "I was the first tornado victim at the hospital." In one of the many ironies of the day, one of the last known injured persons was the first of many to be treated at St. Joseph's.

Hundreds of stories of tragedy, reunion and heroism rose from the destruction that day. In a special tornado edition printed on May 6, 1967, the *Belvidere Daily Republican* wrote in a front-page editorial:

> *Literally hundreds of heroes emerged in the crisis. They responded as only real heroes can, working tirelessly to help others, responding to the needs*

> *of others and ignoring their own needs and their own safety, saving lives, helping to salvage property, helping to restore some semblance of order in the wake of the catastrophe.*

These heroes are yet another example of Boone County originals.

One whose efforts cannot be overlooked is Belvidere police captain Francis "Dutch" Whalen. Many tornado survivors owe their lives to Whalen. To many, the first sound they heard warning them about the impending disaster was not the howling fury of the tornado but a police siren. Whalen was on his typical duty of supervising the exchange of bus riders at Belvidere High School and keeping an eye on traffic as students left the brand-new school for the weekend. He was sitting in his police cruiser a block away from the high school, which had opened earlier in the fall, when he got a radio report from Officer Harry Farris, who said he saw a tornado rip off a corner of the Chrysler plant. Whalen looked to the southwest and spotted the tornado. He reacted immediately. "I turned on the red light and siren and started yelling at the kids to get back into the school building. More than a hundred of them stampeded back into the school."

Marty Prather, a high school student, was in a line of cars waiting to turn onto East Avenue from the school parking lot. All of a sudden, Prather said, "We saw a police car coming up to the end of East Avenue. We figured there was an accident or something or somebody was in trouble." It was Dutch Whalen, siren roaring, lights flashing. He slammed on the brakes in front of the line of cars. "He jumped out of his car and started yelling at the people in the first car and went from car to car."

When Whalen was asked about the tornado, he said, "It was terrible, but it might have been a lot worse if [Officer Farris] hadn't sounded the warning."

Heroes came in all sizes. Mary Ann White, recently married and five months pregnant, was caring for an older woman while her husband, Terry, served in the U.S. Air Force in Turkey. White was talking on the phone when she started to hear objects hitting the house. "All of a sudden, a brick came through the window, so I hung up," she said. White knew the safest place was the basement, but the speed of the storm and the condition of the elderly woman limited her options.

> *I just knew I wouldn't make it back with her to the basement because she didn't understand very much. So, I shoved her under the bed and I tried to crawl under as far as I could, being five months pregnant. [Then] everything came down on us. There wasn't much left of the house I was in.*

# Remarkable People and Curious Incidents

Gary Loofboro and his girlfriend, Stephanie Kokenes, who is now his wife, were on one of only two buses that departed Belvidere High School that afternoon. They saw the tornado from the bus window, and their screams prompted the bus driver to floor the accelerator as the bus sped down State Street. The bus eventually dropped off all of its passengers, and when Loofboro got home, he listened as his father, a part-time deputy sheriff, got a call to come and help at the high school. Loofboro asked his father if he could come along. They drove as far as they could, and when debris closed off all approaches, they walked to the school.

Loofboro was standing near the school entrance when he saw a man he knew, Randall Trueblood. Trueblood was looking for his daughter, who had driven his station wagon to the school. Someone spotted the wagon and asked if it could be used to transport an injured boy to St. Joseph's Hospital. Trueblood asked Loofboro if he would come with him to the hospital. When they arrived, hospital officials told them that they were unable to treat the boy. "They said they were full and that we should take him to Rockford," said Trueblood, who still hadn't located his daughter and didn't want to leave.

He asked Loofboro if he could drive. Loofboro said he could but that he didn't have his license. Trueblood told him, "You take him to Rockford anyway, and away he went." Loofboro said, "I was scared to death. My dad was a policeman and all of that was on my mind." Not only did Loofboro drive to Rockford without a license, but he also went to all three hospitals before he dropped the injured boy off at Rockford Memorial. "I had no idea where I was. I remember stopping at gas stations and asking how to get there. Then I drove the car back to Belvidere. It was wild. I didn't tell my dad about it until it was all over."

Joel Schumacher, acting principal of Immanuel Lutheran School, was in his normal spot after school—outside with teachers watching the eighty or so children who were awaiting their buses. Somehow, perhaps taking note of the dark clouds to the southwest, Schumacher sensed danger. He moved quickly, telling the teachers to round up the kids and get them back inside the school. Some of the teachers had already moved inside and suggested that the children return to their classrooms. But Schumacher said no. "He insisted that they all go down to the basement," said former pastor Eugene Wille, who was a junior pastor at the church in 1967. "All the teachers followed his orders, and they all went to the basement, into the locker rooms where they were safe." In a story that appeared in the *Rockford Morning Star*, Schumacher's wife recalled, "My husband is very storm conscious, and he was sure something bad was coming. He and other teachers got the children inside, and the other male teacher, Thomas McGhee, started them singing to keep their minds off the storm." One of the hymns they sang was "Jesus Loves Me."

After the sounds of crashing and smashing glass faded away, those in the basement walked upstairs into the gym, and the first thing they saw was the sky. One whole section of the gym roof was gone. In one part of the school, three of four classrooms were gone—books, papers and desks all scattered. One of the walls of the kindergarten room had collapsed. It was clear that Schumacher's quick thinking had saved injuries and, most likely, lives. Although the storm killed seventeen children, only one was an Immanuel Lutheran student, and she was killed on a bus at the high school. "Had they gone to their respective classrooms, there is no doubt that many of these kids would have been injured, if not killed," Wille said.

> *Some of those classrooms were directly hit and hugely damaged. [Schumacher] was determined, whether it was insight or a sense of some impending disaster. I would say he was a hero, if you want to call him one, although I never heard anyone say he was a hero. Hindsight is very good when you look back.*

Verna Schwebke was driving to the high school with her six-year-old son, Scott Schwebke, to pick up an older son, Ken. They were in a big wide-track Pontiac, Verna in front and Scott in the backseat, and neither was wearing a seatbelt, a common practice in the 1960s. All of a sudden, Verna pulled the Pontiac sharply into someone's driveway and said, "Oh, my God! A tornado's coming!" When the car screeched to a halt, Verna reached across the front seat and pulled her son into the front, throwing him under the dashboard.

> *And she laid on top of me...I can still remember the car just bouncing. It didn't move, but it went up and down, up and down, up and down. It seemed like the tornado lasted forever, but, obviously, it was a short time.*

When they sat up, they found that all of the windows and headlights were gone, and both were covered in mud. Verna had glass and other debris in her hair and on her back and neck. Scott knows that his mother acted instinctively to protect him that day. "Oh, she saved my life," he said. "I don't think there's any doubt. I would have been torn to shreds."

# Remarkable People and Curious Incidents

Verna's decision to pull into a driveway was fortuitous, and so was the direction she pointed the car—east to west, facing the tornado. "[Had] she pulled into someone's driveway facing [away from the tornado]…I'm sure that we would have rolled the car. She turned right into the storm." When the two lifted their heads and looked outside the car, they were amazed. "We were about fifteen feet from the house," Scott said. "And when we got up, the house was gone. There was nothing left but the first-floor decking; everything was gone. To this day, we're still trying to figure out how we stayed there in that driveway."

Eleanor O'Donnell began her shift as a licensed practical nurse at Highland Hospital at 3:00 p.m. on that third Friday in April. As she got her reports on patients, she noticed that sunlight was peeking through the dark clouds. The next time she looked outside, about 3:50 p.m., it was raining, and a window was open at the end of the pediatric hall. When she went to close it, she was stunned.

> *I saw what looked like dark smoke coming across the vacant lot from Pearl Street. As I looked closer, I saw our garbage shed, which was about the size of an outhouse, [get] picked up whole across the back lot. At the same time, the car directly behind the hospital started circulating up in the air and the garage across the street went airborne.*

Eleanor had to convince herself that what she was seeing was real. "That took about a second," she said. "Then I turned and ran towards the nearest baby." That's when the tornado hit the hospital.

When she tried to open the door to where the baby was, the pressure of the tornado kept it shut tight.

> *The wind rolled me across the wall toward the desk; there were ceiling tiles, books, and toys flying. The noise was like the roar of a hundred trains; you thought your ears could not stand it, and then it was very silent. There was debris everywhere. I ran to the door and pushed it open and the child had slept through the whole thing. There was only dust and dirt on his crib. He was uninjured.*

O'Donnell then began to check on patients she knew were in harm's way. An elderly woman in Room 53 was covered with debris, and large wooden beams were lying on top of her. As she went to get help, she checked on other patients. All were OK, including two women in front rooms who had been in the lobby shopping at the gift shop when the tornado hit. When O'Donnell checked their rooms, she found that large beams had crashed into each bed. Finally, she was able to get help for the woman in Room 53.

About that time, volunteers began to stream into the hospital. One man showed up with an end loader and cleared out the driveway. Then he cleared a path down State Street for a block or two. The hospital had no power, so the workers did what they could. "A couple of ladies took our dressing car and supplies down to the basement," O'Donnell said.

> *We were doing triage in the basement, down in the laundry, which had no power, no lights. The roof from the center wing, our surgical wing, flew off. They said we needed the pharmacy, which was also on our floor. A state cop came along and I said I didn't have the key. He said, "Lady, you want it open?" And he took his foot and kicked the door open.*

Even though the hospital was one of the buildings with serious damage, tornado victims kept showing up, as did others looking for shelter. One other nurse wanted to wash everyone, but there was only "a trickle of water and I didn't know long that was going to last," O'Donnell recalled. "We washed what they had to suture. We were in dire shape at first because we had no doctors."

They were still working in the dark in the basement at 5:00 p.m. About that time, a bus arrived with doctors and nurses from St. Anthony's Hospital in Rockford. Eventually, the most critical patients were evacuated to other hospitals. Kitchen workers showed up with sandwiches and coffee, and by 9:00 p.m., most patients were out of the building. About 9:30 p.m., the hospital closed its doors.

When O'Donnell got to her car, which was undamaged, she realized that that Friday was when the egg lady made her regular delivery. The egg lady had placed seven-dozen eggs in the front seat. Expecting to see an omelet at best, she found that only two eggs had cracked during the storm.

Gary Turner lost all of his top teeth that day but was otherwise uninjured. He lost some cattle, but the house withstood the storm; the barn took the brunt of the damage. Afterward, his fields, like others, were covered with debris, including thousands of fruit cans from a neighbor's junkyard. But people came from near and far to help with the cleanup, including Mennonites from central Illinois. This was indicative of the volunteer effort that Belvidere and Boone County received for the days, weeks and months afterward. "The volunteers came and picked up the fields so we could farm that year," Gary said. "It was unbelievable."

# "Our Miss America"

After the tornado of April 21, 1967, Belvidere and Boone County needed something positive to put them on the map. They got it in a big way on the national stage—on a boardwalk, in fact, one of the most famous in the world. On Saturday night, October 7, 1968, Belvidere's own Judi Ford was crowned Miss America 1969.

"I can't believe it. I just can't believe it," were the first words Judi said after being named Miss America. It was a long journey for the small-town girl, who, in Michael Jordan–like fashion, didn't make her junior high school cheerleading squad.

Judith Ford was the younger of two children born to Virgil and Marjorie Ford. Virgil was a labor relations executive for Sundstrand Corp., a large engineering and manufacturing company in Rockford. Marjorie taught English at Belvidere High School, which both of her children attended, starting with son Don. Judi grew into an accomplished athlete at an early age. When she was eight years old and a member of the local swim team, she announced that she was entering the diving competition the next day. Her family thought she had never even jumped off a board, but she told them she had been practicing. Expecting the worst, the family was amazed when Judi placed third. She continued to practice on the board and became successful, winning most titles in the area.

Over time, Judi came to know what was necessary to succeed and, more importantly, to be a good competitor. In *Sharing the Crown*, a book Marjorie wrote about her successful daughter, Judi said:

# Boone County Originals

Official portrait of Judi Ford, Miss America 1969. *Courtesy of the Boone County Historical Museum.*

Miss America Judi Ford on her throne at the pageant in Atlantic City, 1968. *Courtesy of the Boone County Historical Museum.*

# Remarkable People and Curious Incidents

*Competition is healthy for anyone for a variety of reasons. In addition to helping a person stay physically fit, it teaches sportsmanship, dedication, and the ability to accept failures as well as successes. At the start, you lose more than you win. I know. I would work out for months and months for just one chance in a meet. Then my knees would buckle or I would miss a routine, and it would seem that all was lost. This happened to me plenty of times.*

When Judi was attending Belvidere High School, competition sports were for boys only. Title IX was a few years away, and the only competition for girls, aside from intramurals, was to cheer. Her first cheerleading tryout in the seventh grade was not successful, but she went to all of Belvidere Junior High School's games that year to learn the cheers. She even went to practices and was prepared for tryouts as an eighth grader. Again, she got bad news. That drove her determination as she practiced even more, adding more zip

Photo capturing the moment Judi Ford was named Miss America 1969. *Courtesy of the Boone County Historical Museum.*

to her routine with cartwheels and back flips. This time, she made it, and she cheered for four years at Belvidere High School.

Others began to notice Judi's natural ability, and soon it was suggested that she try the trampoline. It's not much of a leap to go from the diving board to the trampoline, which is taken from the Spanish word *trampolin* for "diving board." In the 1960s, Rockford was a center of trampoline success through the coaching of Robert Bollinger, and Judi blossomed into a champion. Eventually, she focused all of her energy on the trampoline, winning national titles and eventually becoming a member on the U.S. trampoline team at the age of fifteen in 1965. That summer, she and Marjorie traveled to Vienna, Austria, to compete.

About that same time, an opportunity came along for her to enter a queen contest. Her first experience in this new type of competition was at the Boone County Fair in 1966. The county fair is considered by most in Boone County to be the biggest event of the year. For six nights in the second week

Miss America Judi Ford receives an award for her military support. Ford visited Vietnam during the war. *Courtesy of the Boone County Historical Museum.*

## Remarkable People and Curious Incidents

of August, seemingly all commerce and any important activity are moved to Fairgrounds Road north of Belvidere for the Boone County Fair. And the first day of the fair features one of its biggest draws: the Boone County Fair Queen Pageant. Judi was sixteen in 1966 when she entered the fair at the urging of her friends and her brother. To no one's surprise, Judi put forward her best effort and won the crown. That title made her eligible to compete for the Miss Illinois County Fair title in January 1967. Reluctantly, she attended the competition, greatly regretting that she would miss cheering at two important boys' basketball games. Once again, Judi and Marjorie traveled together, this time to Springfield, where they found a wonderfully organized event. And, once again, Judi claimed a crown.

The string of good fortune came to a crushing halt on April 21, 1967, when the tornado struck Belvidere. Judi was about to leave school for the day on that Friday with four friends. They were in a car in the parking lot when one of the girls ran back inside to retrieve her homework. As they waited for her to return, the tornado rocked the car, shaking it violently and breaking the back window. Then everything was still, and the tornado had passed. The Fords considered it good fortune that the girl had returned to school because, had the station wagon left earlier, it might have been squarely in the destructive path.

Every house in the neighborhood was damaged or destroyed, including the Ford home. The summer of 1967 was one of rebuilding for the family and more competition for Judi. She graduated from high school and traveled more than six thousand miles that summer as the reigning Miss Illinois State Fair. In September, she left Boone County to attend the University of Southwestern Louisiana, where she could compete on the trampoline in the school's gymnastic program. There, she became the first woman to win a men's varsity gymnastics letter, as well as the first woman to win a major letter.

Later that year, Leslie Carlson, president of the Boone County Fair Association, arranged for the association to sponsor Judi in the Miss Illinois Pageant in 1968. For her talent, she chose an acrobatic dance and trampoline routine, and she set to work on perfecting a three-minute routine. But there was a snag. During the talent presentation, no one could be with her, meaning that she had to perform without spotters. That scaled down the degree of difficulty, but it was still a workable plan. Judi, now eighteen, placed first in the swimsuit and talent competition and was selected Miss Illinois in June 1968. But a state pageant official left her with a warning. According to Judi, "they said, 'You have three strikes against you: You're too young, too blond, and too athletic. Miss America is not supposed to sweat.'"

In September 1968, the Fords prepared to travel to Atlantic City, the traditional site of the Miss America Pageant. Once again, Judi had to perform without spotters, but her skill was clearly of championship quality. Marjorie began to believe that her daughter could actually become one of the finalists. When Judi won the swimsuit and talent competition, she became a favorite to win it all. The next step was to become one of the five finalists—and the last one named was Miss Illinois. The final part of the competition was to respond to a question. That was one area where she tended to struggle, and her brother had offered the following advice after the Miss Illinois pageant. "Listen fumble-mouth," he told her, "you don't talk first and think afterward. If you ever get a chance to do it again, take time to think about what you're going to say, and then say it."

When Judi's turn came, legendary emcee Bert Parks asked her, "Judi, how do you think you could help people live more peaceably together." Keep in mind, this was 1968, the year of the Tet Offensive in Vietnam when antiwar activism forced President Lyndon Johnson to refuse to run for the Democratic nomination. The nation had endured the assassinations of Martin Luther King Jr. and Bobby Kennedy. In Atlantic City, women were protesting what they perceived to be the antiquated Miss America system. A group of women had to be escorted from the Miss American Pageant hall after they unveiled a sign that read: "Women's Liberation." After Bert Parks asked his question, there was a long moment of silence. Marjorie was aghast, believing that her daughter was fumbling for words. But she wasn't. She smiled, stepped to the microphone and said, "I think a person has to learn that he is no better than his neighbor, that all people are created equal and, therefore, should be given equal opportunity for all things." It was a short, eight-second answer, but it was perfect.

As the nation began to follow the final process, everyone in Belvidere seemed to be glued to television sets. And just when the fourth runner-up was named, the power went out. A storm passed through the area, causing a power outage. One can only imagine the anguish in the county as people waited for the power to return. And it did—just in time to hear that Belvidere's own Judi Ford would be crowned Miss America, the first blond winner since 1961 and only the second from Illinois at the time.

About the time Judi Ford took her first steps down the ramp as Bert Parks sang, "There She Is, Miss America," the folks back home in Belvidere ran out of their homes, got in their cars and had an impromptu celebration on State Street. It was just a prelude the real homecoming Judi would get on Wednesday, October 30, 1968, when Belvidere celebrated its queen.

# Remarkable People and Curious Incidents

Downtown storefronts were decorated in red, white and blue and signs, banners, pictures and more hung from every possible place. All of the state's top elected officials took part in the biggest parade in Belvidere's history. There were one hundred units, including twenty-five floats that depicted various parts of Judi's life. About two hundred police officers helped out the fifteen-man Belvidere Police Department. The parade itself was so long that the first units had reached the Boone County Fairgrounds before the last units had even started. The crowd was estimated at between 35,000 and 100,000 people. And it ended at the place where it had all started for Judi Ford—the fairgrounds.

Judi Ford became a popular ambassador for the Miss America Pageant, for female athletes and women everywhere and, especially, for Belvidere and Boone County. She visited troops in Vietnam and was a member of the President's Council on Physical Fitness and Sports for eight years. Both of her parents have passed away. Judi and her brother both live in Geneseo. She has two sons.

On the morning after the Miss America Pageant in 1968, following a news conference, Judi approached her father and asked, "Well, Dad, what you think of your daughter now?"

Virgil Ford replied, "You know, Judi, that you have always been our Miss America."

# A Major Leaguer

He was a three-sport athlete at Belvidere High School, playing football and basketball and running track. But Fred Schulte's best sport—baseball—was not offered at the school in the second decade of the twentieth century. Despite that fact, Schulte is Boone County's most successful professional athlete, even though not many know of him or that he played against Babe Ruth, faced Dizzy Dean and cooked a dinner for Lou Gehrig.

Schulte was a Belvidere native, born on January 13, 1904, and a natural athlete. He spent most of his younger years playing basketball with local semipro teams such as the Union Club, the IOU Club and the Tebala Shrine Temple team. He began his baseball career in 1924 with Waterloo, Iowa, of the Mississippi Valley League, where he hit a league-leading .368 as a twenty-year-old. Schulte played the outfield, where he was able to use his athletic skills. In his first year, he committed only five errors in 115 games, stole twenty-five bases and hit nine home runs. That got him a promotion to the old Milwaukee Brewers of the American Association, where he hit .347 in 150 games in 1926. The next year, he was in the big leagues.

St. Louis had two major-league teams in those days. The St. Louis Cardinals of the National League had players that eventually became known as the "Gashouse Gang." Schulte played for the American League team the Browns, which would move to Baltimore in 1955 and become the Orioles. Schulte played six years with the Browns and, in an interview with *Belvidere Daily Republican* sports editor Jim Killam, recalled playing crosstown games against the Cardinals. "In 1932, we had three exhibition games against the

BOONE COUNTY ORIGINALS

Major-league baseball player Fred Schulte (right), with two Washington Senators teammates. *Courtesy of the Boone County Historical Museum.*

Yunk's drawing of Fred Schulte. *Courtesy Troy Yunk.*

# Remarkable People and Curious Incidents

Photo taken from a newspaper of Schulte's only postseason home run in game five of the 1933 World Series. *Courtesy of the Boone County Historical Museum.*

Cardinals before the season and we won every one. And that was back when they were winning a lot of pennants."

The leader of the Gashouse Gang was Hall of Fame pitcher Dizzy Dean. "I got a kick out of ol' Diz," Schulte said.

> *He used to throw me real tight fastballs, because he figured I couldn't get around on them. And then he'd always want to cross me up, so he'd come back with a curve ball that would be coming right for my neck before it broke over the plate. Well, one day I hit two doubles off him down the left-field line.*

In 1933, Schulte was reportedly sold to the Washington Senators for $100,000, a huge sum in the midst of the Great Depression. If that was the cost, it was worth it; Schulte helped the Senators win the American League pennant and play in the 1933 World Series. Schulte hit .295 and drove in eighty-seven runs in the Senators' season. On the Fourth of July that year, the Senators swept a double-header from the New York Yankees before a crowd of seventy-two thousand at Yankee Stadium. The Senators won the first game 1–0 when Schulte drove in the only run.

> *In the second game, Gehrig and Ruth both got on base and their second baseman [Tony Lazzeri] was up. They put in Sammy Byrd to run for Ruth. Lazzeri hit one to deep right-center and I took off to where I thought the ball was going to hit the wall. It bounced off the wall to me and I wheeled and threw to [Joe] Cronin, the cutoff man. I guess Gehrig thought I was going to catch the ball because he went back to second to tag up. And here's Byrd right behind him coming around the bases. By the time they both got going, Cronin got the ball and threw to the plate. [Washington catcher] Luke Sewell tagged Gehrig and Byrd one after the other and the game was over. That shows you that the real good players forget where the hell they are once in a while.*

Schulte became friends with Gehrig, once inviting him over for dinner in Washington. Benny Bengough, the Yankees' third-string catcher, said that Gehrig "ate like a horse," so Schulte prepared a big meal.

> *I got him a steak about two inches thick and it weighed about three pounds. Well, Gehrig ate the whole steak and looked around and said, "Somebody's going to suffer tomorrow." And the next day he hit two home runs against us. What a guy he was.*

Schulte also was impressed with a side of Babe Ruth that most people don't give him credit for. "A lot of people didn't think Ruth was a very good fielder, but he was a helluva lot better fielder than anybody gave him credit for. He could go get that ball, and if you tried to take an extra base, he could throw you out."

Schulte was also a key player in one of the last plays of the 1933 World Series. The New York Giants led the series 3-1 on October 6 at Washington's Griffith Stadium. Schulte hit only forty-seven home runs in his eleven years in the big leagues and had only one in the postseason. But his three-run homer in the sixth inning of game five tied the game at 3–3, and that's where the score stayed until the top of the tenth inning. The bases were empty when Mel Ott hit a long shot to deep center field, where Schulte was positioned. Schulte turned to follow the ball and came up against a temporary waist-high green fence that had been built on the field to accommodate the overflow of fans. Schulte turned to his right, stretched as far as he could and made a grab for the ball as he fell over the fence. Ott believed Schulte caught the ball and pulled up at second base for what would have been a ground-rule double. Umpire Charles Pfirman first ruled that Schulte had caught the ball but then reversed his call and declared it a home run. Ott trotted home to put the Giants ahead, 4–3, and they closed out the ninth inning and became World Series winners.

Schulte played two more years with the Senators and then two with the Pittsburgh Pirates before leaving the big leagues. He managed minor-league baseball teams in the 1940s and finished out his career scouting for the Cincinnati Reds, Chicago White Sox, Cleveland Indians and the major-league Milwaukee Brewers. He died on May 20, 1983.

# More Boone County Originals

Local historian George Gibson said, "He may have been the smartest man ever to live on Boone County." His name was Montelle Boyd, and if his name is unfamiliar to you, it's because he never made much news outside of Capron in eastern Boone County. It is there that he made news as a locally famous newsman.

Boyd printed the *Boone County Courier*, a truly small-town newspaper that was in circulation for forty years. Boyd was born in the central Illinois community of Kappa and graduated from Harvard University. After college, he returned to Illinois to take a job as a milk tester. Boone County had many creameries in the 1920s, and Boyd tested milk until he got a taste for printer's ink. In 1930, he bought the *Nutshell* from Elmer "Bert" Cramer, who began printing it in 1921 out of Poplar Grove. The newspaper was so small that Cramer's wife, Nora, said that you could fit "all of the news in a nutshell." In 1923, Cramer moved his newspaper to Capron, where he bought a new press that could print a larger edition.

When Boyd bought the *Nutshell* in 1930, he renamed it the *Boone County Courier*, and its staple of news was about who went where and with whom, births, marriages and deaths, church suppers and the like. Boyd also realized that his publication was a forum where he could present new and different ideas. One of his favorite topics was cooperatives, which was logical because he worked in the dairy industry, known for its milk cooperatives. Although there wasn't much interest outside of Capron, Boyd continued to let his voice be heard. One of his successes was the People's Credit Union, and of course, the other was a newspaper that had a forty-year run.

BOONE COUNTY ORIGINALS

*This page*: Two views of Pettit Chapel in Belvidere Cemetery, designed by legendary architect Frank Lloyd Wright. *Photos by author.*

# Remarkable People and Curious Incidents

Another Boone County original, known as "Auntie Wright," delivered babies, dispensed medicine and took care of the sick and elderly in northwestern Boone County in the late nineteenth century. But Cornelia Hayden Wright never attended medical school. The daughter of original settlers, who were among the original settlers of Leroy Township arriving in 1842, she married Gibson Wright in 1855 and settled in a large house west of Blaine. The Wright home was known for its beautiful flower gardens. Twice a week in the summer, she would take bouquets of flowers to nearby Sharon, Wisconsin, and put them on the 7:00 a.m. train to Chicago. From there, they were sent to the Deaconess Home and the Methodist Hospital. The flowers were shipped without charge because packages that weighed less than fifteen pounds were shipped free.

This was a time when rural healthcare was in great need, and at some point, Auntie Wright began to tend to those in need. She was quite intelligent and probably learned much about medicine from reading journals. Local histories tell of her grabbing her black medical bag and being whisked along the roads by her brother, John Hayden, in his white horse and buggy. Some speculate that she mostly dispensed herbs, but she was known to consult a physician in Sharon. Auntie Wright donated books and bookcases for a library in Blaine, where she was also involved with the school and the Methodist church. Not much is known about her because women of that era accepted their positions with dignity. Reverend J.T. McMullen, writing in the *Blaine and Hunter Historical Recorder*, said:

> *Everyone who knows anything about Mrs. Wright knows there is nothing she abhors more than praise or notoriety, but we think it is not befitting that such a life of usefulness should be allowed to pass unnoticed. It would be impossible to tabulate all the good things Mrs. Wright has done in the community. It is not exaggeration to say that there is scarcely a home for miles around that has not, in some way or other, been helped by this beneficent [woman].*

Small in size, Blaine has a lot of history, including Benjamin Bowman, a Pennsylvania native who arrived in Boone County with his brother, Elijah, in 1841. Bowman was a well-known abolitionist during the Civil War and lost five sons and one son-in-law in the conflict. Three of the soldiers are buried at the Blaine Cemetery. When the war began, three Bowman boys were old enough to fight for the Union cause, and the younger ones joined them when they came of age. The first to die was Elijah, named after his uncle. When

Benjamin Bowman heard of his son's injuries, he rushed to be by his side. He was too late to see his son before he died, but he did accompany his body back to Boone County.

Others contributed in their own ways, such as William Streeter, who came to Round Prairie with his brother, Jacob, in 1838 and eventually settled in Blaine. William Streeter was blessed with a wonderful voice, which he used often for services at the Methodist church in Blaine. In those days, it was uncommon for rural churches to have instrumental music, so William performed the roles of organ, organist and choir. "He was a gifted singer and for a number of years took the lead in this very important part of God's work and thus won a permanent place in the hearts of many," Reverend McMullen wrote in the *Blaine and Hunter Historical Recorder*.

A beloved Iowa doctor who passed away at the age of forty-eight and a world-famous architect are unlikely characters in the story of one of Boone County's most famous landmarks, the Pettit Chapel, located on the grounds of the Belvidere Cemetery. The structure is the only memorial chapel that Frank Lloyd Wright designed in his lifetime. If not for the work of a local women's organization, it could have fallen into ruin.

William H. Pettit was born on September 3, 1850, in Boone County, where his father, Daniel, was the principal of Belvidere Academy. William's first career choice was as an educator, like his father, but he loved the idea

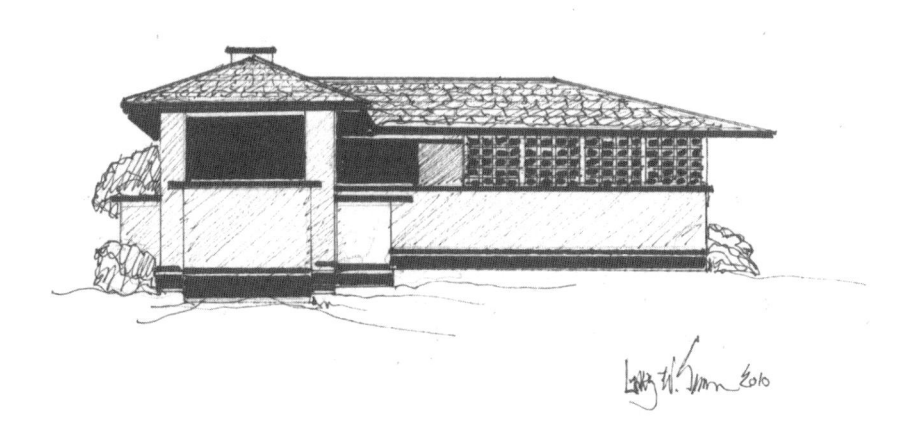

Simon's drawing of the Pettit Chapel. *Courtesy Gary Simon.*

of becoming a doctor, so he went to medical school. Upon graduation in 1874, he moved to Cedar Falls, Iowa, to begin his medical practice. He was successful from the beginning, building a strong, secure practice that was said to be the largest in Iowa, and advancing his profession by joining several medical boards. He also tried his hand in politics in the Republican Party. He married a Belvidere woman, Emma Glasner, on May 9, 1877, and for unknown reasons, they were not able to have children.

On March 25, 1899, after twenty-seven years of service to patients from Iowa to Belvidere, Dr. Pettit died of a heart attack in Cedar Falls. The news of his death was reported in newspapers across northern Iowa and northern Illinois. So many people from Cedar Falls planned to attend his funeral that a special train was chartered from the Iowa City to Belvidere and back. Pettit was buried at Belvidere Cemetery on March 28, 1899.

Mrs. Emma Pettit was grief-stricken and saddened by the loss of her husband and sought to leave a suitable memorial in the community where Dr. Pettit had grown up. She happened to be acquainted with Frank Lloyd Wright, who designed a summer home for her brother, William Glasner, in a northern Chicago suburb. The home had attracted considerable attention for its design and layout, which were uncommonly bold and futuristic for the time. In 1905, Mrs. Pettit and her niece, Helen Keator, visited Wright at his Oak Park, Illinois office, and they were delighted by the architect's ideas and designs. The next year, the Belvidere Cemetery Association approved a plan to set aside a space on the cemetery grounds for a chapel to allow for mourners to pay their respects to their lost family members and friends without having to worry about inclement weather.

In May 1907, work began on the Pettit Memorial Chapel, described in the *Belvidere Daily Republican* as a "handsome structure…Its cost will be about $3,000 and it will be of irregular shape and design." Considered to be one of Wright's earliest examples of his Prairie style, it featured a parlor with a large red brick fireplace and walls of yellow pine and enclosed cypress wood porches at one end, each with large openings. The chapel would be used for funeral services, while the porches would help shelter mourners from adverse weather. The chapel was a gift to the cemetery association and was described in the *Daily Republican* as a "generous, timely, handsome, and practical gift to the association and [the] public [and] will be deeply appreciated, as well for its value as the spirit which prompted it."

For a while, the chapel did serve its purposes as intended by Mrs. Pettit, who left the cemetery association $500 in her will for maintenance and care of the chapel. But in time, funeral homes began to become more popular for local families. They were larger—Pettit Chapel was 17½ by 29 feet—and could hold more people and chairs. The chapel was ignored and fell into disrepair. The cemetery association used it for storage and as a toolshed, and the weather damaged the roof so much that it sagged. Vandals broke windows, including the stained glass, and time caused the porch's floorboards to rot. What was once a gleaming memorial and gathering place for funerals in Boone County had become an eyesore.

Wright died in 1959, and members of his school began to revisit many of his buildings, including Pettit Chapel. Although many of his works were restored, the chapel didn't make the list. There were other efforts at restoration, including one by the Boone County Bicentennial Committee in 1976, but nothing happened until the Belvidere Junior Woman's Club took on the restoration project in 1977. In the spring of that year, the group met with the Belvidere Cemetery Board and got permission to start on restoration. Its goal was to raise $50,000—seventeen times the original cost of the building—and received a $25,000 grant from the Historical Preservation Grants-in-Aid Program. The remaining funds came from local groups, companies and organizations.

The renovation was extensive because of the years of neglect. The brick chimney had to be redone using stucco plaster; the original wood trim was replaced. Although the stained-glass windows were destroyed, old designs showed window patterns to allow for replacement. All aspects were redone, including the installation of bathrooms, as well as gas, electricity and water. The renovation took four years to complete, and the rededication took place on June 8, 1981. The day was significant as it was Wright's birthday and almost seventy-four years to the date that he completed the original chapel.

On the day of the dedication, women's club members told reporters that it was an "effort to not only to return a useful building to its full life, but also enhance the cultural awareness of the town's and world's citizens."

An earlier story told the tale of army general Winfield Scott. He led troops from Chicago to Wisconsin to chase Black Hawk and his band during the Black Hawk War of 1832, a route that was followed by early pioneers and one that reportedly crossed the Kishwaukee River at its most northerly bend in Boone County. Scott's Army Trail, a street in Belvidere, is said to be on the route the soldiers took. A short distance from the street, at the bend of the Kishwaukee, is the site of one of the county's most famous events, which occurred on July 19, 1922. On that day, a gifted athlete and future movie star performed an exhibition at the Marshall Park Beach, which had opened a year earlier.

# Remarkable People and Curious Incidents

A Belvidere street sign acknowledging Scott's Army Trail. *Photo by author.*

The beach was named for George Marshall, who leased the land to the Belvidere Park District for recreational purposes. On the banks above the river were a bathhouse, a concession stand and a log cabin for the lifeguards. On the river below were two piers that were connected by logs. Each pier had a diving board. Just how Johnny Weissmuller came to swim in the Kishwaukee River on that day is not clear. What is clear is that hundreds of people gathered to watch him swim the one-hundred-yard freestyle and perform a diving show. Weissmuller swam at the 1924 and 1928 Olympic games—in Paris and Amsterdam, respectively—winning the hundred-meter freestyle in each, as well as swimming a leg on the four-by-two-hundred relay. He set twenty-eight world records, and his record for the hundred-yard freestyle set in 1927 wasn't broken for twenty-seven years. Weissmuller was one of the first athletes to take his success to Hollywood. He starred in six *Tarzan* films for MGM, but for one summer day, his star shone over Boone County.

Locals who recalled Weissmuller's appearance tell that the river was not very sanitary in those days. Residue, such as corncobs from the nearby canning factory, floated in the water. The health concern eventually

John Lawson with other members of his band. *Courtesy of the Boone County Historical Museum.*

prompted the park district to close the beach and build a pool in Belvidere Park in the 1940s.

John Lawson made sure that no child was tardy to the old Pearl Street School. Lawson was the custodian of the school, which also served as South Side High School and Washington School before being converted into senior citizen housing. Before he rang the bell to start school, he would look up and down the street to make sure that all of the students were inside. He made sure that even the slowpokes were not tardy. John Lawson worked for thirty-nine years at that job and became a beloved figure. It was an amazing journey for a black man born into slavery who fought for the Union in the Civil War.

Lawson was born a slave in Roanoke, Virginia, in 1829 and recalled that as a young boy, serving as houseboy for his master, John P. Taylor, he often served dinner to President Woodrow Wilson's father, Joseph R. Wilson, a friend of the Taylors. Lawson left that household when he was sold to the Killabrew family in Nashville, Tennessee. When Lawson informed his mistress of his desire to join the Confederate army, she arranged for maids to knit three pairs of socks and weave two blankets for him. Lawson had no intention of helping the South. Instead, he stole a mule and escaped to the North, where he joined the Sixteenth U.S. Colored Infantry. Later, he wrote to his mistress to apologize for his deeds and to thank her.

After the war, Lawson followed a Captain Sidell to Belvidere and, for a while, worked for Sidell and his sons on their farm. But when the family

# Remarkable People and Curious Incidents

John Lawson with his granddaughter. *Courtesy of the Boone County Historical Museum.*

John Lawson with the faculty of the Pearl Street School. *Courtesy of the Boone County Historical Museum.*

## BOONE COUNTY ORIGINALS

John Lawson with children from the Pearl Street School. *Courtesy of the Boone County Historical Museum.*

John Lawson, wearing his Civil War medals. *Courtesy of the Boone County Historical Museum.*

moved to California, Lawson remained in Boone County, finding work on another farm on Stone Quarry Road. Dr. Whitman arranged for Lawson to become custodian at the Pearl Street School, where he stayed for nearly four decades. Once, he was working outside the school when he saw a small child playing on the nearby railroad tracks just as a train was approaching. He ran to the boy and grabbed him just before the train rumbled by.

The love that John Lawson had for children was reciprocated when he was surprised at the school play that the children staged at the old Opera House. At the end of the evening, the students presented him with a check for $500 and a round-trip train ticket to Roanoke, Virginia, to visit a brother he hadn't seen in forty-eight years.

A history of Boone County would not be complete without inclusion of Emmett and Bessie Sullivan. The siblings were influential in organizing the Boone County Historical Society Foundation, as well as its museum, and left trust funds for other local organizations. The Sullivans moved from Iowa

## Remarkable People and Curious Incidents

to Belvidere before the turn of the twentieth century, and over the years, Emmett and Bessie became well-known merchants who operated Sullivan's Department Store in downtown Belvidere. Emmett was a natural leader. He made the first radio in Belvidere and set up the first radio manufacturing facility. A veteran of World War I, he served on the local draft board during World War II. His interests were wide; not only did he help preserve land for Kinnikinnick Conservation Area, but he and Bessie also found one of the last remaining models of the Eldredge Runabout in Pennsylvania and arranged to purchase it and donate it to the historical museum. Emmett was influential in securing the building in which the Boone County Historical Museum currently resides.

One of the treasured items in the museum's collection is a silent movie filmed locally in 1926 called *Belvidere's Hero*. Financed by the *Belvidere Daily Republican* and the Rhinehart family, it told the story of how a local boy rescued a girl. All of the players were from Belvidere, and locations included the old Chicago and North Western Railroad Station, the State Street Business District, the Rhineharts' former home and various locations in and around Big Thunder Park. Many of the interior shots were filmed on the stage of the Apollo Theatre after the regular evening performances. Audience members delighted in watching the film crew set up cameras and film while they looked on.

The climax of the film was a great auto crash in front of the old post office. Mayor Harry Gabel furnished the Hudson and Essex cars for the scene. Not surprisingly, Gabel was Boone County's Hudson and Essex dealer. The premier was held at the Apollo Theatre on March 31, 1926, and it was a memorable event. After several showings, the film was forgotten until several museum society members remembered it. Emmett Sullivan was one of those members and was able to find film cans and have them restored.

Emmett Sullivan died in 1981 at the age of eighty-five. He had no children but had a soft spot for youngsters nonetheless. During America's bicentennial celebration in 1976, Emmett arranged for all of Belvidere's children to receive a free ice cream cone at the Dari-Ripple. The idea to do this came from his childhood. When he was about eight years old, he went to the YMCA, where he handed over a quarter and asked for membership. When told the fee was three dollars, Emmett was disappointed but not discouraged. He saved money from his paper route and paid off the fee in installments, even though the YMCA had no such payment program. Years later, when he was a successful businessman, he told his sister, Bessie, that someday he would like to buy every youngster in town a free ice cream cone.

So he arranged for the YMCA to distribute a ticket for a free ice cream cone at the Dari-Ripple.

Bessie died five years later and left lasting funds to support the museum, the Belvidere YMCA, the Belvidere Cemetery Association and Ida Public Library. She shared her brother's vision to preserve Boone County for future generations and helped to acquire land for Kinnikinnick Conservation District. She followed the exchange in ownership in significant historic local homes and made sure that the new owners were aware of their homes' histories. Before Bessie died in 1986, she paid tribute to her brother when Belvidere celebrated its sesquicentennial. On June 8, 1986, she offered to buy an ice cream cone for every area child, ten years old and younger. Coupons were available at United Bank, Belvidere Bank, Ida Public Library and the YMCA. Bessie told the *Belvidere Daily Republican* that she did it in memory of her brother.

In his poem, "The 1936 Belvidere Blowout," local hobo sage Hairbreadth Harry described a gathering of what he called "rambling rounders." Harry also wrote several lines on those who helped provide food for the gathering, including "Billy Piel." Belvidere's "King of the Hobos" had a special liking for the merchant as he wrote in the poem, "Piel's Store":

> *What makes Piel's Store so crowded*
> *When other stores keepers loaf?*
> *It may be William's talent*
> *Maybe his tact or both.*
> *What makes Piel's Store so crowded*
> *What gives the magic note?*
> *It must be his smile so cheery*
> *Says Hairbreadth Harry the poet.*

W.H. "Billy" Piel opened Piel's Grocery Store in 1890 on South State Street after working as a clerk in another retail grocery store. In the July 1926 issue of the *Country Gentleman* magazine, Piel said that after working for more than four years, he had amassed $450. "By the advice of a Monarch salesman, I was encouraged to go into business for myself," he said. "I opened my store May 10, 1890."

Piel wasn't satisfied to be just another retailer in downtown Belvidere. To set himself apart from other merchants, he began buying in large quantities. He was the first retail grocer to buy a full carload of Monarch coffee, and consumers became aware of the bargains. Once customers bought forty

## Remarkable People and Curious Incidents

thousand pounds of Monarch coffee in forty days. One of greatest public relations successes came in 1935, when he bought a giant wheel of cheese. Encased in wood, the cheese arrived at the railroad station, where it was unloaded and then rolled up the street to Piel's. There it was opened, and pieces were put on sale. It was gone in a week.

At its peak, Piel's employed about fifty men and women as managers, clerks, deliverymen, telephone operators and office workers. It was not unusual for sales to ring up more than $5,000 a day during the deepest days of the Great Depression. The store's impact was noticed by the magazine, which reported, "Belvidere is a flourishing town because it enjoys a splendid trade with farmers from twenty miles around who go there to buy their groceries [from] W.H. Piel."

Looking at downtown Belvidere today, it is difficult to imagine the large crowds that could be found at Piel's on State Street. Another difficult concept to imagine is that most of the farmers and their families came into town on Saturday night. The weekdays were for work and chores; Sunday was a holy day. On Saturday, you got your chores done quickly, spruced up and went downtown to Belvidere, where the sidewalks were crowded with shoppers at places like Sullivan's Department Store, which was run by Emmett and Bessie Sullivan. Sullivan's Department Store started small in 1938, but over the years, it expanded to include ladies', children's and babies' clothing; books; gifts; sewing machines; and other electrical appliances. The store eventually expanded to include two storefronts on two floors.

Other popular merchants were George Ames's dry goods store, Loncor's Drugstore, meat markets run by the Bingenheimers and Livermores, Kelton's ladies' store and Wheeler and Slater for men's clothing. If you needed hardware, there was Thrush's and Heywoods, and if it was news or a good cigar you needed, you went to the Hub. Many kids got ice cream at Smith and Rend's Pool Hall. After World War II, the downtown landscape began to change as Schultz Brothers and J.C. Penney's drew many shoppers. Across the street was Lear's Jewelry Store, run by Bob and Ruth Lear. It was down the block from Belvidere Bank, a local institution that was formerly known as Farmers National Bank.

Belvidere Bank became the largest bank in Boone County through the work of Hugh K. Funderburg, who came to Belvidere in 1911 to manage the Keene-Belvidere Canning Company. Funderburg, an Ohio native, worked summers at canneries to finance his college education. That experience brought him to Belvidere, where he became one of the most influential figures of the twentieth century. He saved half of his $100 monthly salary, ate only two meals a day and purchased enough stock in the company to take it over. In 1944, he sold the plant to Green Giant, which continues to operate at the site today under the ownership of General Mills. Funderburg was involved with Farmers National Bank for thirty-eight years, moving up to eventually become chairman, and he also served as chairman of K-B Farms, one of the largest agricultural landholders in the county.

Belvidere's best-known podiatrist probably was Dr. Richard Sandburg, who died at the age of ninety in 2005. Sandburg was a tireless supporter of civic affairs and was once awarded the Doctor of Civil Betterment Award by the Belvidere Area Chamber of Commerce. A more interesting note about him was that he was the nephew of famous poet Carl Sandburg. Both were born in Galesburg, Illinois, and Richard Sandburg was proud of his relative. He often lectured about the Pulitzer Prize–winning writer and had three bookshelves of his work, including four volumes of *Abraham Lincoln: The War Years*. That is the work for which Sandburg received the Pulitzer Prize.

Carl Sandburg visited his nephew once in Belvidere in 1959 at his home on Caswell Street. While the famous Sandburg was admiring some pine paneling in the basement, Richard's wife asked him if he would like a drink. Sandburg requested a boilermaker and a helper. When he realized the Mrs. Sandburg didn't know what he was asking for, Carl said, "Just mix some bourbon with a beer and set up another beer on the side." Sandburg, eighty-one at the time, spilled some beer on a table and stained it. Later, when Richard Sandburg sold some of his furniture, one prospective buyer pointed out the stain on the table. When he was told it came from Carl Sandburg's spilled drink, the man said, "I'll take it!"

Pulitzer Prize–winning writer Carl Sandburg on a visit to Belvidere. His nephew, Richard Sandburg, is at right. *Courtesy of the Boone County Historical Museum.*

# Remarkable People and Curious Incidents

Many other names and businesses have come and gone. Two of the most enduring names involve automobiles. Manley Motors has been selling cars since 1898 and is the second-oldest Ford dealer in the United States. The Wolf brothers—John and Jack—have been selling cars on Belvidere's west side for years.

As described, people have been moving through and into Boone County for centuries.

The first large-scale immigration came in the 1840s, when the county was still being settled, and these new residents were Norwegian. The first group came about 1840 and settled in the rolling and wooded hills of northwestern Boone County, which would become Manchester Township. They came to farm, and that's what one of the original settlers, Eric Duxstad, did. Duxstad homesteaded 120 acres before acquiring another 40, paying $1.25 an acre for the original land. Local history describes Eric's wife as a true original. Eager to learn English, she walked to Beloit College, eleven miles away, several times a week to learn the language. She did her part on the farm, too, which was covered with timber, helping to cut the trees and dig out the stumps so the land could be farmed.

It has been said that many of the first Norwegians to settle in Boone County were actually on their way to Minnesota, where many other people from their country settled. But when these settlers saw the land in northern Boone County, they decided to stay. Another early Norwegian settler was Ole Rong Tillerson, who came in 1846. His parents, three brothers and two sisters followed him about two years later. Ole found land on Jefferson Prairie, built a log cabin and walked to Dixon to claim his land, for which he also paid $1.25 an acre. Ole paved the way for many other Norwegians to follow, helping to finance their journeys and getting them established.

Ole had a large family, and one night his two-year-old son apparently wandered away. The family frantically searched and went to bed without finding him. The next morning, a neighbor about a mile away noticed a flock of sheep huddled in the pasture. When he approached the sheep, he was surprised to find a sleeping little boy. The sheep had huddled around the boy overnight to keep him warm and safe.

Another Norwegian immigrant was Ole K. Natesta, who had planned a wedding. But when he tasted food cooked by his fiancée, he shipped her off to another family, the Tuttles, and told her, "As soon as you can cook as good as Mrs. Tuttle, I'll marry you."

The Irish were the next immigrants to make an impact in Belvidere, following the Norwegians a few years later. But something else brought them to Boone County: the railroad. The Galena and Chicago Railroad that came from Chicago meant jobs—hard, backbreaking jobs—but to one of the country's newest group of immigrants, it meant a start. When William Holt Gilman gave the railroad the right of way on the south side of the Kishwaukee, he knew that the land that was called "the flats" wasn't worth much and would stay that way if the railroad were on the other side of the river.

Even with the railroad, the land wasn't worth much, so it was a natural place for the Irish to start their lives when the railroad brought them there in the 1850s. The area they settled is hard by the river, a ten-block area bounded by East Pleasant Street on the south, Main Street on the west, Meadow Street on the North and Gilman Street (named after the early entrepreneur) on the east. It was truly on "the other side of the tracks," as it was located between the river and the railroad tracks. Gilman also donated land for a Catholic church, St. James, which was built at the corner of Church and Caswell Streets. It was a short walk over the tracks to church for the Irish people, whose neighborhood became known as the Irish Patch.

Hispanics were the third major immigrant group to come to Boone County, arriving in the early twentieth century. The first Spanish surnames appear in local census records in 1920, and among the early family names entered were Larango, Delgardo and Venegas. It's not known if they were true immigrants or simply had Spanish names. Most of the earliest Hispanic people to move to the area were farmworkers who followed the crops. K-B Canning hired many workers during the canning season, and many of them were Hispanic. Over time, many returned to the area, found it to their liking and put down roots. And like the Norwegians, Irish and other immigrant groups, other family members followed.

The first documented Hispanic family to come to Boone County followed a route carved out by the Irish immigrants. Manuel Martinez is believed to have headed the original Hispanic family, and the railroad brought him here. Martinez worked for the Chicago and North Western Railroad, arriving in Boone County in the late 1920s or early 1930s from Mexico. They lived on McKinley Avenue, and his children were the first Hispanics to enroll in public school in Boone County. The family lived here for a short time, eventually moving to Rockford during World War II. Each of these and other immigrant groups has had a lasting impact on the county.

Such impacts will be made by all of us Boone County Originals in many ways. And the future will give us even more of them.

# Bibliography

The majority of information for this book comes from columns written for the *Rockford Register Star* from June 1995 to early 2010. In addition, information was gathered from classes taught and handouts provided by the late Roger Gustafson of the Boone County Conservation District and George Gibson of the Boone County Historical Museum. This list contains additional sources.

Bateman, Newton, and Paul Selby. *Historical Encyclopedia of Illinois and History of Boone County*. Chicago: Munsell, 1909.

*Belvidere Daily Republican*, April 23, 1901; May 3, 1906; December 2, 1911; July 2, 1935; November 9, 1971; June 30, 1978; February 24, 1981; May 21, 1983; March 29, 1996.

*Belvidere Illustrated*, 1896.

*Belvidere Standard*, November 22, 1853; November 29, 1853; April 11, 1882; August 28, 1883.

Blanton, DeAnne. *Women Soldiers of the Civil War*. Baton Rouge: Louisiana State University Press, 1993.

Boone County Bicentennial Commission and Boone County Conservation District, comp. *Boone County Historic Trail Map*. 1976. Updated reprint by

# BIBLIOGRAPHY

Boone County Sesquicentennial Steering Committee, Boone County Conservation District and Illinois Office of Tourism, 1985.

Boone County Historical Museum. Unpublished historical essays, 1997.

*Boone County Independent,* January 1883.

Bowley, Bessie. "Young People's History of Boone County and Belvidere." Unpublished document, 1958.

Davis, James E. *Frontier Illinois*. Bloomington: Indiana University Press, 1998.

Doyle, Amanda M. "Pettit Memorial Chapel: Through the Years and How It Stands Today." Unpublished paper, 1998.

Doyle, Mike. *The Belvidere Tornado, April 21, 1967: A 40-Year Perspective*. Belvidere, IL: Boone County Historical Society, 2007.

Ford, Marjorie. *Sharing the Crown*. Litchfield, IL: Publication Investments, Inc., 1971.

Franck, Fred. *Landmarks: The Story of Boone County*. Belvidere, IL: Boone County Heritage Days Committee, 1835–1985.

Hall, Homer. *Flora: The First Hundred Years*. N.p., 1973.

Hall, Richard. *Patriots in Disguise: Women Warriors of the Civil War*. New York: Paragon House, 1993.

Hallstrom, Herbert. *Flora: A History of South Prairie*. N.p.: self published, 1976.

Hodge, Frederick Webb. *Handbook of American Indians North of Mexico*. New Haven, CT: Human Relations Area Files, 1975.

McMullen, Reverend J.T. *Blaine and Hunter Historical Recorder*. Sharon, WI: Reporter Print, 1906.

Meacham, Jon. *American Lion*. New York: Random House, 2008.

# Bibliography

Millett, Allen R., and Peter Maslowski. *For the Common Defense: A Military History of the United States of America*. New York: Free Press, 1994.

Moorhead, Virginia B., ed. *Boone County: Then and Now*. Belvidere, IL: Boone County Bicentennial Commission, 1976.

*Past and Present of Boone County, Illinois*. Chicago: H.F. Kett and Co., 1877.

Radebaugh, William. "Boundary Dispute Between Illinois and Wisconsin." *Proceedings of the Chicago Historical Society* (1904).

*Rockford Register-Gazette*, May 31, 1907.

Rowland, Katherine E. *The Pioneers of Winnebago and Boone Counties Who Came Before 1841*. Baltimore, MD: Gateway Press, 1990.

*Survey of Sculpture in Boone County*. Belvidere, IL: Boone County Arts Council, 2009.

Tanner, Helen Hornbeck. *Atlas of Great Lakes Indian History*. Norman: University of Oklahoma Press, 1987.

Way, Royal Brunson. *The Rock River Valley*. Vol. III. Chicago: S.J. Clarke, 1926.

Webber, Muriel. *Boone County Heritage Days '78*. Belvidere, IL: Boone County Heritage Days Committee, 1978.

Wood, Wales. *A History of the Ninety-Fifth Regiment Illinois Infantry Volunteers*. 1865. Reprint, Boone County Historical Society, 1993.

Yurs, Mark E. *Wheels of Change: Essays in Boone County History*. Belvidere, IL: Boone County Heritage Days Committee, 1989.

# Websites

Abraham Lincoln Historical Digitization Project. Northern Illinois University. http://lincoln.lib.niu.edu.

# Bibliography

Baseball-Reference.com. www.baseball-reference.com.

Boone County Historical Museum. www.bchmuseum.org.

Chicago and Northwestern Historical Society. www.cnwhs.org.

Farm Collector. www.farmcollector.com.

International Sewing Machine Collectors Society. www.ismacs.net.

Miss America Organization. www.missamerica.org.

Ryder, Stephen P., and Johno. "Dr. Thomas Neill Cream, 1850–1892." Casebook: Jack the Ripper. http://www.casebook.org./suspects/cream.html www.casebook.org.suspects.cream.html.

Wikipedia. www.wikipedia.org.

# Index

**A**

Ames
  Albert T. 74, 75
  George 49, 50
  Sarah T. 74, 75
  William 49
Armour, John 28

**B**

Banks, George 54
Big Thunder 11, 20, 33, 34, 40–42
Blackford, Charlotte 35
Black Hawk 21–22, 124
Bliss, Daniel 29, 30
Blood, Arthur 24, 69, 73
Boone, Daniel 11, 14
Boyd, Montelle 119
Bradford, William 37
Butler, Mark I 83

**C**

Cady
  Alvah 30–31
  Catherine 30–31
Carlin, Thomas 45
Carlson, Leslie 109
Case, Candice 29, 30
Cashier, Albert 55–60
Chamberlain, Catherine 53
Clausius, Gerhard P. 57
Cline, Cornelius 23–24
Coone, R.W. 73
Crawford, Frank 10, 59
Cream, Dr. Thomas N. 73
Cronin, Joe 116
Crosby, Nathanial 35, 38–39

**D**

Davis, Jefferson 21
Dean, Dizzy 113, 115
Doty
  Edward 37
  Hannah Shaw 37
  Judge J.D. 44, 45
  Simon P. 11, 13–14, 35, 37–39, 41–42, 47, 74
  Solomon 37
Douglas, Stephen 61
Dunham, David 23
Dunton
  George 74
  Nellie 73–74
Duxstad, Eric 133

# Index

Dysart, Hugh R. 83

## E

Eldredge, Barnabus 85–86, 88, 90, 91
Emerson, R.H. 53

## F

Farris, Officer Harry 100
Ford
  Don 105
  Judi 105–111
  Marjorie 105, 109, 110
  Virgil 105, 110
Fuller
  Allen 47, 55, 61, 65–66
  Ida 65–66
  Nancy Benjamin 65
Funderburg, Hugh K. 131–132

## G

Gabel, Mayor Harry 129
Gehrig, Lou 113, 116
Gibson, George 119
Gilkerson, William 53
Gilman, William Holt 27, 47, 52, 134
Glasner, William 123
Goodhue, Dr. Josiah 35, 38–40
Gould
  Ira 33
  Jared B. 33, 35
Grant, General Ulysses 57, 62
Greenlee, John 28
Gregory, Janette 28

## H

Hairbreadth Harry. *See* Moan, James Joseph
Hall, Devillo 13
Handy, John 25, 26
Harvey, Daniel 28
Hayden, Ormond 74
Hodgers, Jennie. *See* Cashier, Albert
Hononegah 28
Hoover, Herbert 54

Hovey, T. Adelbert. 66
Humphrey, Colonel Thomas 60
Hurlbut, Stephen 47, 55, 60–65, 71

## I

Ives, Charles W. 57–59

## J

James, Jesse 69, 70–71
Jenner, Asher 22, 39
June, F.T. 86, 88

## K

Keator, Helen 123
Killam, Jim 113
Kokenes, Stephanie 101

## L

Langdon, John 23
Lannon, Mrs. Patrick 58
Lawson, John 126–128
Lazzeri, Tony 116
Lear
  Bob 131
  Ruth 131
Leister, Edward 37–38
Lincoln, Abraham 21, 45, 60–62
Lish, Senator Ira 58–59
Loofboro, Gary 101

## M

Mack, Stephen 28
Marshall, George 125
Martinez, Manuel 134
Metcalf, Archibald 23
Moan, James Joseph 14, 77–83, 130

## N

Natesta, Ole K. 133
Neff, Harold 89
Nixon, Erastus 23–24, 42

# Index

## O

O'Donnell, Eleanor 103–104
Ogden, William 47
Ott, Mel 116–117

## P

Parks, Bert 110
Peck, Ebenezer 35, 38, 39
Pepper, Samuel 58, 59
Pettit
  Dr. William H. 122–123
  Mrs. Emma 123
Piel, W.H. (Billy) 130–131
Pope, Nathanial 43
Powell, John 70
Prather, Marty 100

## Q

Quinn, Pat 54

## R

Radebaugh, William 43, 44
Ralston, Gavin 53
Rhinehart, Frank 67
Rice, Walt 29, 30
Robbins, Livingston 23
Rollins, John Quincy 27
Ruth, Babe 113, 116

## S

Sandburg
  Carl 132
  Dr. Richard 132
Sawyers, General James 27
Schulte, Fred 113–117
Schumacher, Joel 101–102
Schwebke
  Scott 102–103
  Verna 102–103
Scott, General Winfield 22–23, 29, 124
Sewell, Harold 83
Shattuck, Erastus 26
Standish, Myles 37

Stott
  Daniel 71–73
  Mrs. Stott 71, 73
Sullivan
  Bessie 69, 128–131
  Emmett 69, 128–131
  Henry 69–71
  John 69–71
  Rose 69, 70
  Timothy 69, 70

## T

Thiebeau, Joseph 18
Tillerson, Ole Rong 133
Towner
  John K. 23, 24, 35, 38
  Mrs. Towner 24, 38
Turner, Gary 97, 98, 99, 104
Tuttle, Lundy 63, 64

## W

Weissmuller, Johnny 125
Whalen, Captain Francis (Dutch) 100
White, Mary Ann 100
Whitman
  Dr. Frank 71, 128
  Seth 47
Whitney, Dr. Daniel 35, 38, 39
Wilson
  Joseph R. 126
  Woodrow 126
Wolf
  Jack 133
  John 133
Woods, Wales 60
Wright
  Cornelia 121
  Frank Lloyd 122–124, 124

## Y

Younger
  Bob 70
  Cole 70
  Jim 70

# About the Author

Mike Doyle teaches high school journalism and social studies in Belvidere, Illinois. He is a member of the Boone County Historical Society and served six years as a museum board member, one as vice-president. Mike is a National Board Certified Teacher in social studies and is a member of the Journalism Education Association. He has conducted sessions on writing and reporting at local, regional and national conventions. He graduated from the University of Wisconsin–Whitewater, where he majored in geography and minored in history. He received his master of arts in teaching and leadership from St. Xavier University in Chicago.

Visit us at
www.historypress.net